Early Childhood Mathematics Activities

Author
Denise LaRose, M.A.Ed

Credits

Publishing Credits

Dona Herweck Rice, *Editor-in-Chief*; Lee Aucoin, *Creative Director*; Don Tran, *Print Production Manager;* Timothy J. Bradley, *Illustration Manager*; Jodene Smith, M.A., *Editor*; Leslie Huber, M.A., *Assistant Editor;* Robin Erickson, *Interior Layout Designer;* Corinne Burton, M.S. Ed., *Publisher*

Shell Education
5301 Oceanus Drive
Huntington Beach, CA 92649-1030
http://www.shelleducation.com

ISBN 978-1-4258-0699-6

Reprinted 2013

Table of Contents

Introduction and Research

Today, more than ever, greater demands are being placed on classroom teachers to teach children all the various dimensions of mathematics. Educators are guided by national, state, and local mandates to ensure that students become successful in mathematics. Much research has been done linking successful implementation of standards to game playing (Moss, 1997; Perry, 1997). These mandates apply to all students, including young learners as they enter preschool and kindergarten. The key to teaching these emergent learners is to provide a balanced program that is developmentally appropriate. *Early Childhood Mathematics Activities* is a resource that can be useful to you as a classroom teacher while you guide students in meeting these mandates.

The games in this book are divided into four categories: **shapes and patterns, identifying numbers, counting, and adding and subtracting**. Most of the activities and games are intended for small groups, but can be modified for larger groups. Each game has a list of suggestions or adaptations that allow the games to become more flexible based on the needs of your classroom. When working with small groups, remember to utilize parent volunteers. The more involved a parent is with his or her child's education, the more successful that child will be. What better way for a parent to be involved than to actually help in the classroom by working with a small group? Once students understand the rules and procedures, less adult supervision will be needed and students may even be able to play by themselves.

But why play games? It has been suggested that if more children played fun, educational games, there would be fewer adults with math fears. Much has been written about math fears, as well as the impact they have on learning (Burns, 1998). By creating a safe, positive environment, math fears diminish. Children can achieve success in math by learning in a fun and enjoyable environment (Buehler, 1992). This positive environment must meet the mathematical needs of students while providing playful activities (Guha, 2000). The environment should consist of playing games and having children actively involved in fun activities (Onslow, 1990; Willoghby, 1981; Kanter, 1999). It has often been thought that children learn best through play (Allen, 1979). Many parents understand this, and if you walk into any preschool or kindergarten classroom, you will discover this to be true. Unfortunately, some children who enter school without game-playing experience have difficulty learning math in school (Wakefield, 1997). It then becomes the role of teachers to help students develop an understanding and love of mathematics at an early age. And what better way to do this than to play games? **Activities and games are much more fun and achieve better results than worksheets and drills (Summer, 1994; Goldberg, 1990). Children construct mathematical understanding through the form of play** (Burk, 1992).

This book will complement any mathematics program you are currently using. The goal is for children to gain a basic understanding of mathematics concepts while having fun. Your students will enjoy the games and learn to love mathematics! Have fun playing!

How to Use This Book

Selecting Activities and Games

The activities and games in this book are divided into four sections: **shapes and patterns**, **identifying numbers**, **counting**, and **addition and subtraction**. See the table of contents for the specific page numbers on which sections begin. Begin by reviewing the activities and games by the skill you want; however, do not be limited by the sections. Many of the activities and games in this book can be adapted to any of the skills listed. For example, the activity "Gum Ball Machine" is in the Identifying Numbers section of the book; however, the activity can easily be adapted to have students practice addition or subtraction. Suggestions for adaptations are provided at the bottom on the teacher direction pages.

Preparation and Storage

The materials needed for each activity or game are listed on the teacher direction pages. Specific patterns or game boards that may be needed are on the pages following the teacher directions. The patterns can be photocopied in black and white from this book and then colored by hand, or they can be **printed in full color from the interactive whiteboard-compatible teacher resource CD**. Glue the pieces to construction paper or thin cardboard to create more durable pieces. Consider laminating all the pieces for durability, too. Enlarging the patterns and game boards is another option you may wish to consider. Use a copy machine with an enlarge option or copy the pattern onto a transparency. Place the transparency on an overhead projector and trace the image onto a piece of poster board.

A 9" x 12" (23 cm x 30 cm) manila envelope with a clasp works well to store most of the pieces needed for each game. You may want to create an envelope for each game in order to keep the pieces organized and easy to access. Be sure to clearly label each envelope with the name of the game. Once the materials needed to play the game are gathered and the game pieces created, preparation for the activities and games is minimal. Consider photocopying the teacher-direction page and cutting out the "Activity Procedures." Glue these procedures to the front of the manila envelope. These directions tell how to do the activity or to play the game. The envelope can be handed to a parent volunteer or classroom aide. Only minimal verbal directions will be necessary because everything needed is contained within the envelope.

How to Use This Book (cont.)

Introducing the Activities and Games

Even though many of the games are designed for a small group, you may wish to introduce the activities and games in a whole-class setting. You may have to select a few students to help you demonstrate how to do the activity or play the game, or you may be able to modify the activity slightly in order to accommodate the whole class. An overhead projector, document camera, or interactive whiteboard are other methods of introducing an activity or game to the whole class. Photocopy necessary patterns onto transparencies, which can then be projected on a screen for the whole class to see. Finally, the activities and games can be introduced in a small group. Be sure to consistently describe and play the game with each group. When the children play the game independent of teacher supervision, you will want all of them to play by the same rules. Consider your class and the particular activity to decide the best method of introducing the games to your students.

It is useful to remind students each time an activity or game is introduced or played that the purpose is to practice math concepts, not to see who can win. Everyone wins if math concepts are learned and practiced in a fun way. You may wish to make it a policy that everyone gets a sticker, "kudos" from the teacher, or other small prizes if they participate in the activity or game. This reinforces the fact that everyone is a winner when he or she practices math.

Parent Volunteers and Classroom Aides

Utilize parent volunteers and classroom aides to assist you in preparing the materials in this book. Often, parents who are unable to volunteer in the classroom are willing to assist in coloring or assembling materials that are sent home. Be sure to provide directions and all of the materials necessary for the volunteers to complete the task. Providing a "return by date" also helps you get the materials back in a timely manner.

Parent volunteers, classroom aides, and cross-age tutors are excellent resources for monitoring small groups as they play games. Provide game monitors with directions on how the activity is to be done or how the games are to be played. Remind the monitors that the purpose of the activity or game is to practice math.

Who Goes First?

Who goes first? This is probably one of the most contested questions when children play games. You will want to have this question answered prior to introducing an activity or game to the students. You may wish to have a set procedure that can be used for determining who goes first for all the activities and games, or you may wish to select a different procedure for each activity and game. Either way, having the procedure established will eliminate many arguments. Some suggestions for determining who goes first are listed below.

- Roll a die.
- Draw straws.
- Pull numbers out of a "hat."
- Flip a coin.
- Play rock, paper, scissors.
- Choose the person wearing the most blue (or any other color).
- Select the youngest/oldest.
- Have ladies/gentlemen go first.
- Have students play in alphabetical or reverse alphabetical order.

Observing Students for Assessment

Take advantage of the great opportunity to assess students as you observe them participating in math activities or playing math games. There are a variety of assessment tools, such as checklists, anecdotal notes, and data-capture sheets that can be used for documenting observations. Data-capture sheets are especially helpful to document events, behaviors, and skills that can be used to provide an overall picture of what a student is capable of, and areas in which the student still needs to develop. Data-capture sheets usually incorporate a checklist of specific behaviors to be observed and space for observation notes. Below is a general form that can be used as you observe students participating in math activities and games. The first two observations are general observations that can be applied to almost any activity or game. Fill in the bottom two observations to include specific skills to observe, such as "Displayed an understanding of less than one."

Y = Yes, behavior exhibited S = behavior somewhat exhibited N = behavior not exhibited

Student Name ______________________________ Date__________________

	Y	S	N	
1.	❑	❑	❑	Exhibited an adequate understanding of the activity/game.
2.	❑	❑	❑	Displayed knowledge of math vocabulary related to the activity/game.
3.	❑	❑	❑	____
4.	❑	❑	❑	____

Overall, the student's performance [circle choice] expectations...

went beyond met overall met partial met minimal did not meet

Notes:

Standards Correlations

Standards Correlations

Shell Education is committed to producing educational materials that are research and standards based. In this effort, we have correlated all of our products to the academic standards of all 50 states, the District of Columbia, and the Department of Defense Dependent Schools.

How to Find Standards Correlations

To print a customized correlation report of this product for your state, visit our website at **http://www.shelleducation.com** and follow the on-screen directions. If you require assistance in printing correlation reports, please contact Customer Service at 1-877-777-3450.

Purpose and Intent of Standards

The No Child Left Behind legislation mandates that all states adopt academic standards that identify the skills students will learn in kindergarten through grade twelve. While many states had already adopted academic standards prior to NCLB, the legislation set requirements to ensure the standards were detailed and comprehensive.

Standards are designed to focus instruction and guide adoption of curricula. Standards are statements that describe the criteria necessary for students to meet specific academic goals. They define the knowledge, skills, and content students should acquire at each level. Standards are also used to develop standardized tests to evaluate students' academic progress.

Teachers are required to demonstrate how their lessons meet state standards. State standards are used in development of all of our products, so educators can be assured they meet the academic requirements of each state.

McREL Compendium

We use the Mid-continent Research for Education and Learning (McREL) Compendium to create standards correlations. Each year, McREL analyzes state standards and revises the compendium. By following this procedure, McREL is able to produce a general compilation of national standards. Each lesson in this product is based on one or more McREL standards. The chart on the following page lists each standard taught in this product and the page numbers for the corresponding lessons.

Standards Correlation Chart

Standard	Benchmark	Activity/Game & Page	
Standard 2 Understands and applies basic and advanced properties of the concepts of numbers (Grade: Pre-K)	2.1 Understands that numbers represent the quantity of objects	Cookie Numbers.......84–89 Give a Dog a Bone ... 90–93	Feed the Monkey ...... 94–101 Ladybug Match......... 106–111
	2.2 Counts by ones to ten or higher	Action Numbers........ 68–73	
	2.3 Counts objects	Apple Picking .... 74–79 Colorful Giraffe.......... 80–83	High Dots.................. 102–105 Ladybug Match......... 106–111
	2.4 Understands one-to-one correspondence	Apple Picking .... 74–79 Colorful Giraffe.......... 80–83	Make Ten 116–119
	2.5 Understands the concept of position in a sequence	Missing Number....... 120–127	
	2.6 Knows the written numerals 0–9	Complete the Clock ... 34–37 Find Your Partner ...... 38–39 Gem Dig .... 40–43 Gum Ball Machine.... 44–47	Mail Carrier .... 48–51 Number Match .... 52–57 Number Walk............ 58–59 Short Racers 60–65
	2.7 Knows the common language for comparing quantity of objects (e.g., "more than," "less than," "same as")	More and Fewer .... 112–115 Make Ten 116–119	
Standard 3 Uses basic and advanced procedures while performing the process of computation (Grade: K-2)	3.1 Adds and subtracts whole numbers	Jump the Line............ 128–129 Add One .... 130–133 Bull's Eye! .... 134–135 Number Ducks .... 136–145 Pepperoni Plus.......... 146–149	Disappearing Stars... 150–151 The Big Scoop .... 152–155 Parachuting............... 156–159 Egg Carton Shake..... 160–164
Standard 5 Understands and applies basic and advanced properties of the concepts of geometry (Grade: Pre-K)	5.1 Knows basic geometric language for naming shapes (e.g., circle, triangle, square, rectangle)	Color My World .... 10–13 Silly Pumpkin .... 14–17 Robot Builder............. 18–21	
Standard 8 Understands and applies basic and advanced properties of functions of algebra (Grade: Pre-K)	8.1 Understands simple patterns (e.g., boy-girl-boy-girl)	Colorful Caterpillars... 22–25 Pattern Race............. 26–27	Ice Cream Scooper ... 28–31 Edible Jewelry 32–33
	8.2 Repeats simple patterns	Colorful Caterpillars... 22–25 Pattern Race............. 26–27	Ice Cream Scooper ... 28–31 Edible Jewelry 32–33

Color My World

Skill:

Recognizing shapes

Suggested Group Size:

2–6 students

Activity Overview:

Students color a shape in a picture according to the shape that is displayed.

Materials:

- "Color My World – Version A" (page 12)
- "Shape Cards" (pages 166–168)
- markers or crayons

Activity Preparation

1. Photocopy "Color My World – Version A," one per student (or print copies from the CD).
2. Photocopy "Shape Cards" on card stock paper.
3. Cut out the cards.
4. Laminate the cards for durability.

Activity Procedure

1. Provide each student with "Color My World" and markers or crayons.
2. Show one shape card at a time to the students. As you show each card, have the students identify the shape.
3. Have the students look at their pictures to find and color the matching shape. Students may color the shape as many times as it appears in the picture.
4. Continue showing the shape cards until the students have colored all of their pictures.

Adaptations

- Repeat the activity using "Color My World – Version B" (page 13).
- Have the students look throughout the room for items with the same shapes as are on the cards. Also, discuss shapes that can be found in the environment.
- Have the students use a pencil and write an X on the shapes they find in their pictures as each shape card is shown. Students may color their pictures at a later time.
- Allow the students to color only one shape in their pictures per card shown. Place each shape card under the deck after its use so that the cards are used repeatedly and the activity can continue until everyone has colored his or her picture.

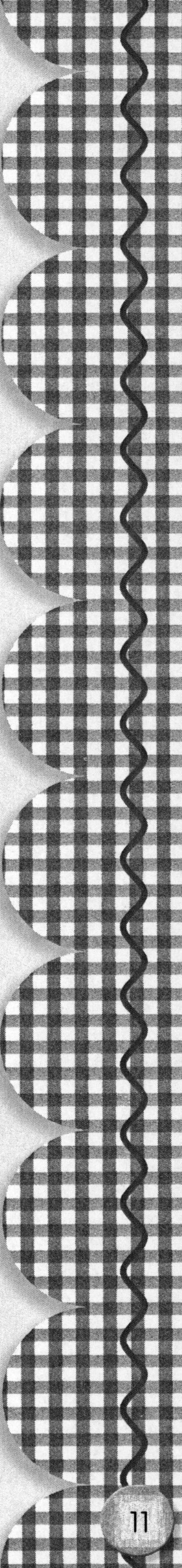

Color My World – Version A

Color My World – Version B

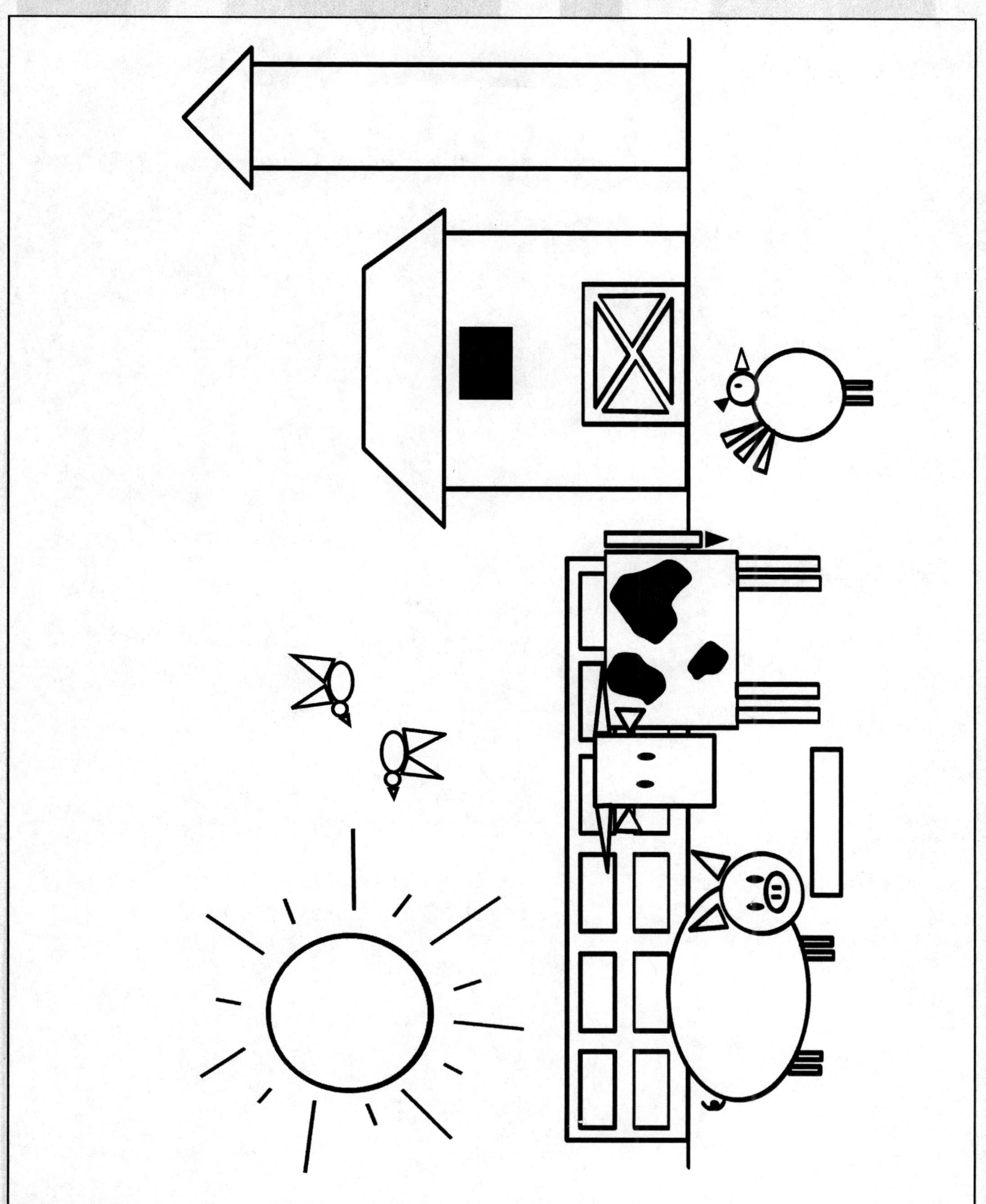

Silly Pumpkin

Skill:

Recognizing shapes

Suggested Group Size:

2–6 students

Activity Overview:

Students place shapes on pumpkins that match shapes on cards.

Materials:

- "Pumpkin Face" (page 16)
- "Face Features" (page 17)
- "Shape Cards" (pages 166–168)
- glue sticks

Activity Preparation

1. Photocopy "Pumpkin Face," one per student, (or print color copies from the CD).
2. Photocopy "Face Features," one per student (or print copies from the CD).
3. Cut out the shapes on "Face Features."
4. Photocopy multiple sets of "Shape Cards" on card stock paper.
5. Cut out the shape cards.
6. Laminate the shape cards for durability.

Activity Procedure

1. Give each student a pumpkin.
2. Shuffle the shape cards and place them face down in a central location.
3. Place the face-feature shapes in a central location.
4. Tell the students they will be using the shapes from the face-feature shape pile to create faces on their pumpkins.
5. Have a student take the top card from the shape card deck and identify the shape. If the student correctly identifies the shape, he or she can select the matching shape from the face-features shape pile and keep it. If the student cannot identify the shape, then the next player can take his or her turn.
6. Allow the student to decide which feature on the pumpkin (i.e., mouth, nose, eyes, ears) he or she wants the shape to be. The student can then glue the shape into place on the pumpkin.
7. Have other students take turns following the same procedure. The activity is over when all the pumpkins have complete faces.

Adaptations

- Have the students draw the shapes instead of using the shape patterns.
- Wait to glue the shapes in place until the end of the activity. Allow the students to move the shapes around before gluing.
- Use white paper and let the students color the pumpkin and shapes.

Pumpkin Face

Face Features

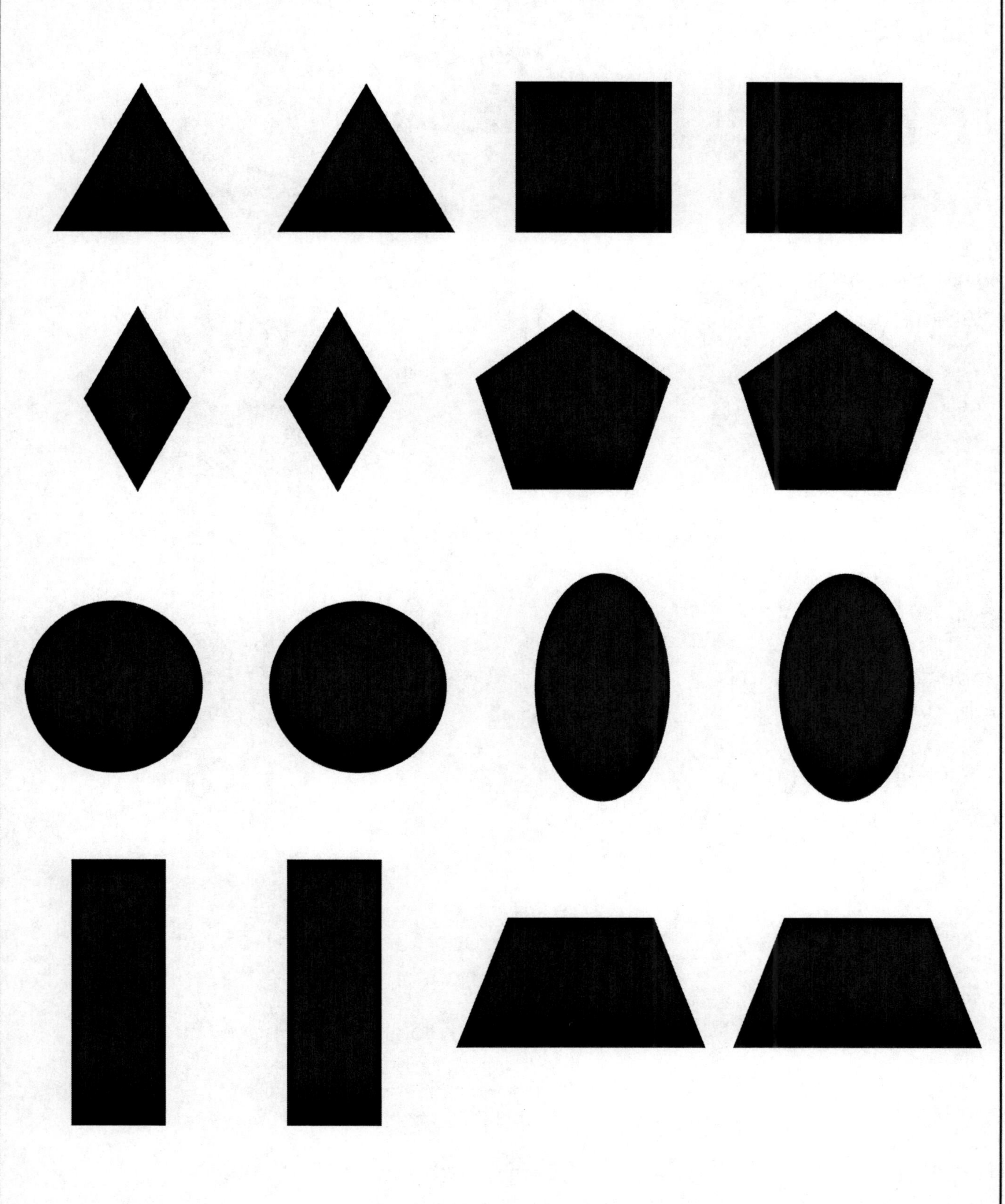

Robot Builder

Skill:

Recognizing shapes

Suggested Group Size:

2–6 students

Activity Overview:

Students use shapes to build a robot.

Materials:

- "Robot Picture" (page 20)
- "Shape Cards" (pages 166–168)
- crayons or markers

Activity Preparation

1. Photocopy "Robot Picture," one for each student (or print copies from the CD).
2. Photocopy four sets of "Shape Cards" on cardstock paper.
3. Cut out the cards.
4. Laminate the cards for durability.

Activity Procedure

1. Give each student a robot picture.
2. Place the shape cards facedown in a pile in a central location.
3. Ask a student to take the top card from the deck of cards.
4. Have the student show the group the card and identify the shape. The student then colors an example of that shape on his or her robot.
5. Return the shape card to the bottom of the card deck.
6. Have other students take turns following the same procedure. If a card that a student does not need is turned over, he or she may select another card. The activity is over when all the robots have been colored or "built."

Adaptations

- If a student turns over a card that he or she does not need, the student waits until it is his or her turn again before turning over another card.
- Instead of using the shape cards, use the 0–3 number cards (pages 168–169). Each time a student turns over a number card, he or she can color that many shapes on his or her picture.
- Provide each student with "Robot Shapes" (page 21). Have the students cut out the shapes and design their own robots.

Robot Picture

Robot Shapes

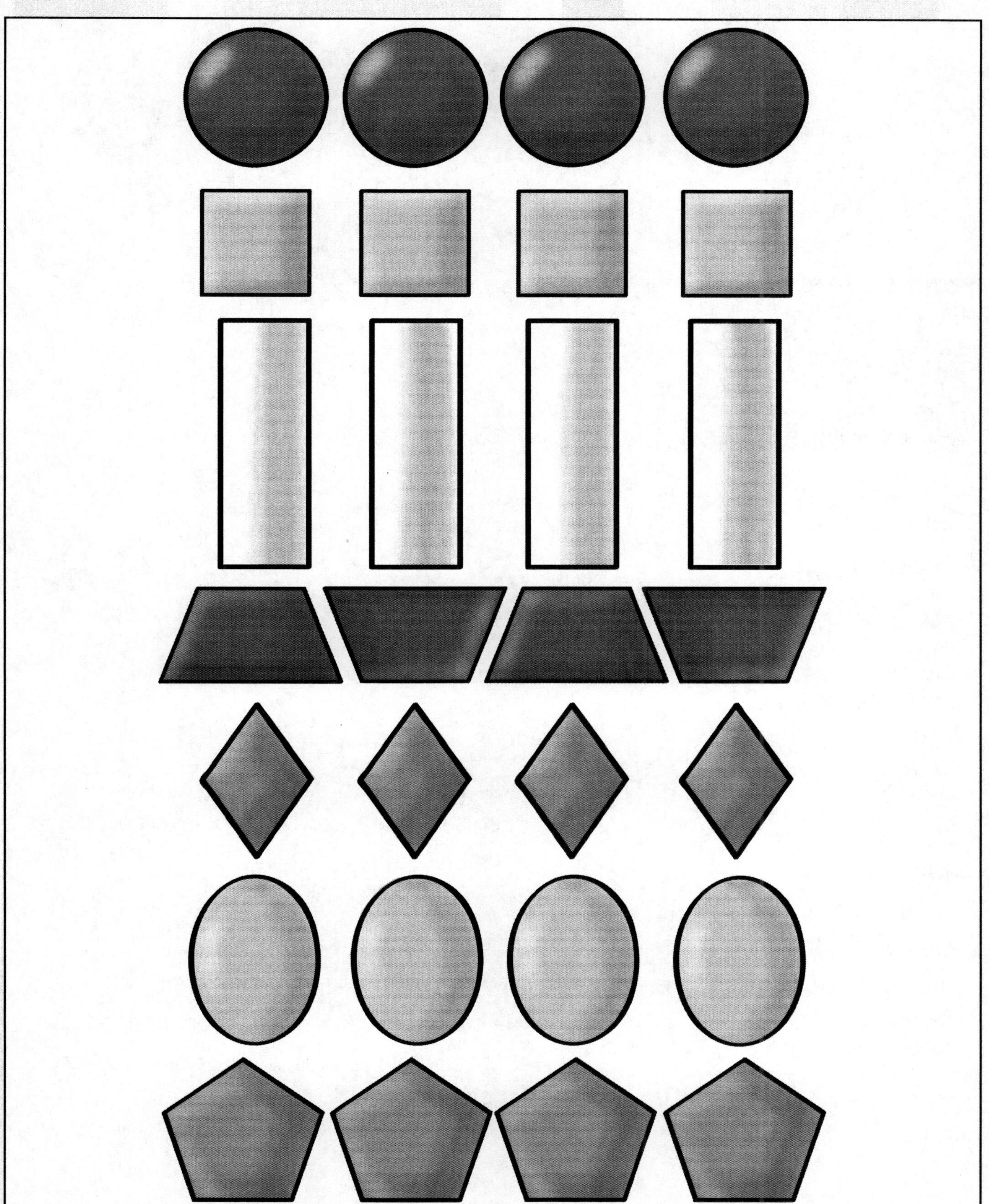

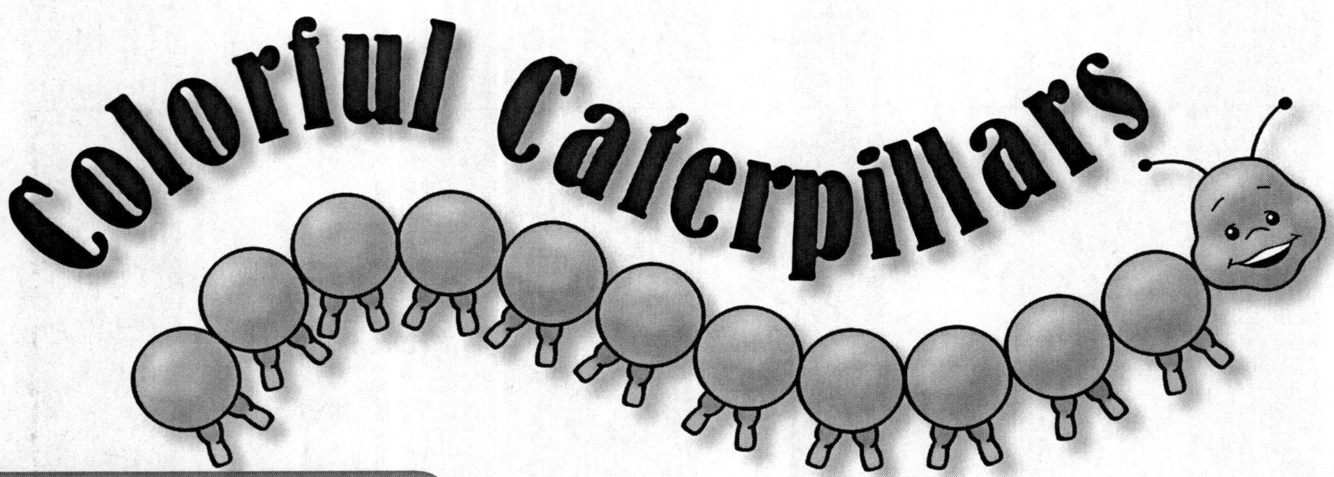

Skill:

Creating patterns

Suggested Group Size:

Whole class

Activity Overview:

Students color a caterpillar to create a pattern.

Materials:

- "Caterpillar Pattern" (page 24)
- crayons or markers
- materials for creating a pattern (See Activity Procedure #2.)

Activity Preparation

1. Photocopy "Caterpillar Pattern," one per student (or print copies from the CD).
2. Create visual examples of patterns for students to reference. Listed below are a variety of materials that can be used to illustrate patterns for the students.

- Snap together connecting cubes.
- Draw circles and squares on the board.
- Glue die-cut patterns on a sheet of paper.
- Set out school supplies, such as pencils and erasers, on the desk.

Activity Procedure

1. Review with the students what a pattern is. Remind them that a pattern repeats in a predictable way.
2. Show the students visual representations of patterns. Discuss the various patterns.
3. Draw a caterpillar on the board and have a student color the body of the caterpillar to demonstrate a pattern.
4. Give each student "Caterpillar Pattern" and markers or crayons.
5. Have the students color the caterpillar to show a pattern.
6. Allow the students to share their patterns with the group when they are finished.

Adaptations

- Provide the students with "Caterpillar Shapes" (page 25). Have the students cut and glue shapes onto each of the circles of the caterpillar to create a pattern with shapes.
- Have the students write letters in each of the circles of the caterpillars to create letter-pattern caterpillars.
- Have the students write numbers in each of the circles of the caterpillar to create number-pattern caterpillars.

Caterpillar Pattern

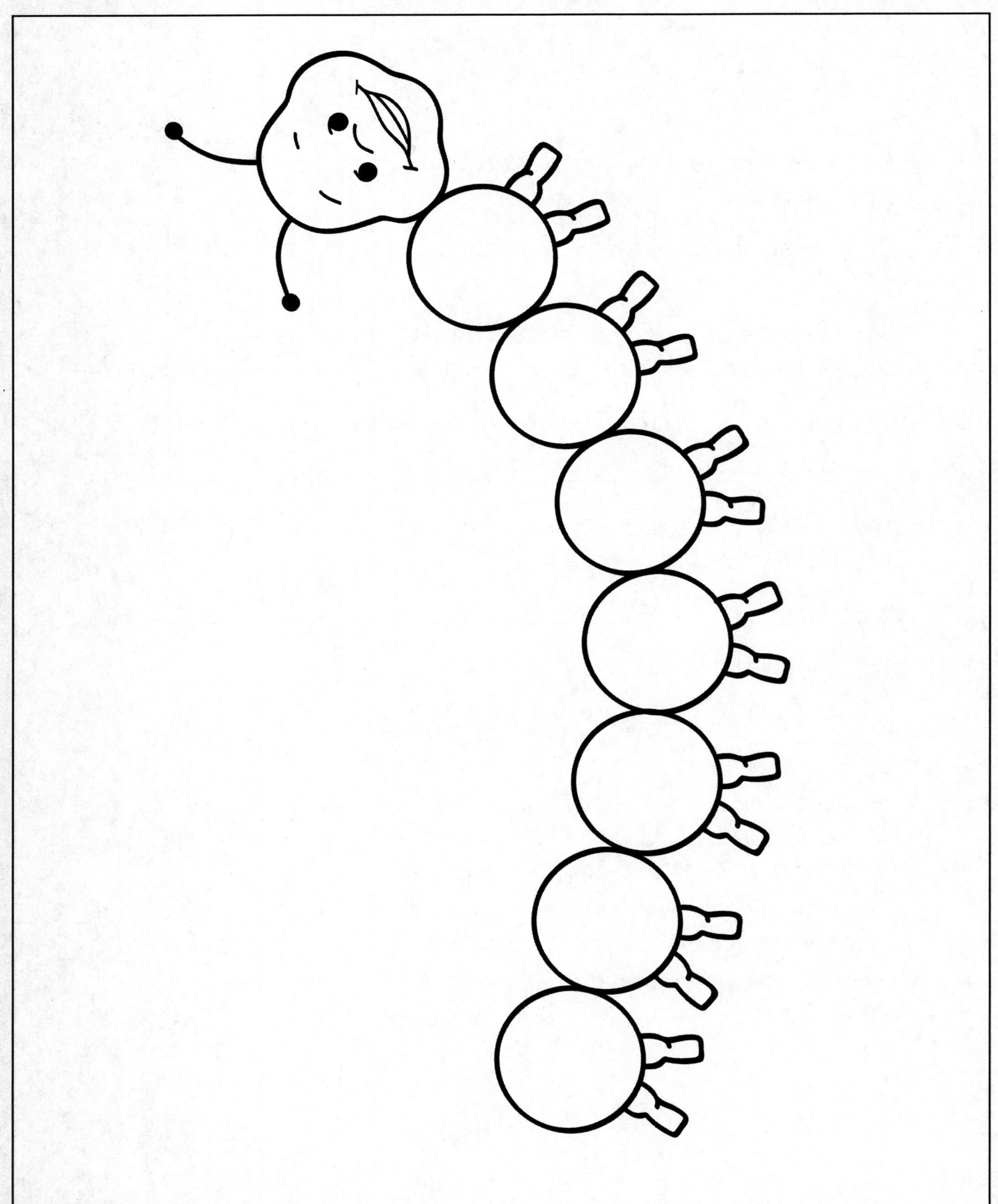

Caterpillar Shapes

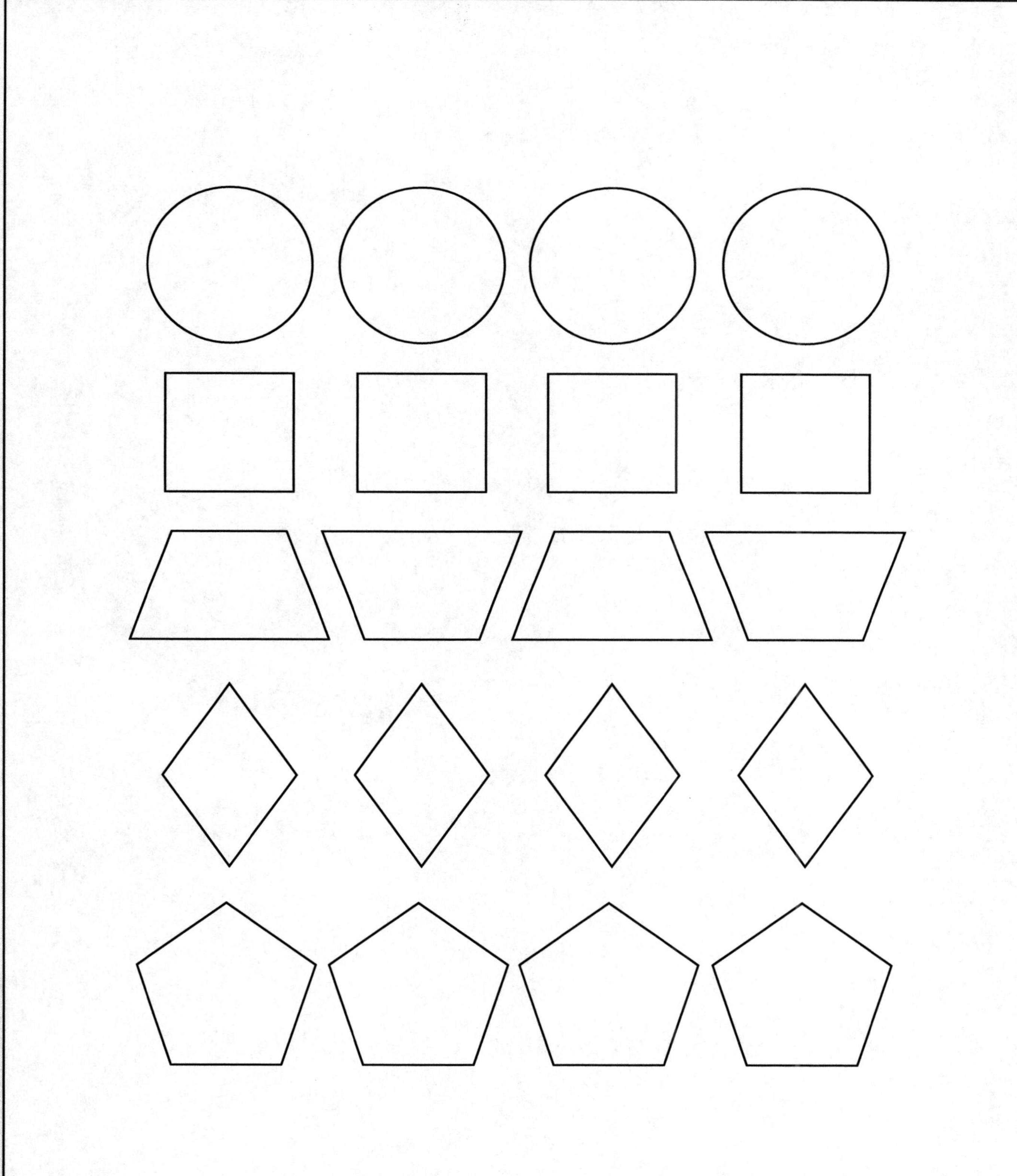

Pattern Race

Skill:

Creating patterns

Suggested Group Size:

2–4 students

Activity Overview:

Students race against the clock as they create patterns using number cards.

Materials:

- 0–6 "Number Cards" (pages 168–170)
- egg timer or a watch with a second hand

Activity Preparation

1. Photocopy multiple sets of 0–6 number cards on cardstock paper.
2. Cut out the cards.
3. Laminate the cards for durability.

Activity Procedure

1. Sort the number cards into like groups so that all the cards with the same number are together, and place them faceup in a central location.
2. Review with the students what a pattern is. Remind them that a pattern repeats in a predictable way.
3. Set the timer for one minute.
4. Have pairs of students work together to create a number pattern within the time limit. Students may use any combination of number cards to create the pattern.
5. Ask pairs of students to share their patterns and tell how many times the pattern repeats.
6. Have other students follow the same procedure.

Adaptations

- Use the shape cards (pages 166–168) instead of the number cards.
- Shorten or lengthen time as needed.
- Challenge students to create complex patterns (for example, AABB or ABBCCCDDDD).
- Limit the numbers that are used; for example, use only 0–3 number cards.
- Increase the amount of numbers that are used; for example, use 0–8 number cards.

Skill:

Creating patterns

Suggested Group Size:

2–6 students

Activity Overview:

Students create patterns by coloring and organizing scoops of ice cream.

Materials:

- "Ice Cream Cone Pattern" (page 30)
- "Ice Cream Scoop Patterns" (page 31)

1. Photocopy "Ice Cream Cone Pattern," one per student, on cardstock paper, and color as desired (or print copies from the CD).
2. Cut out the ice cream cones.
3. Laminate the ice cream cones for durability.
4. Photocopy multiple copies of "Ice Cream Scoop" patterns on various colors of cardstock paper (or print color copies from the CD) so that each child can have 6–10 scoops of ice cream.
5. Cut out the ice cream scoops.
6. Laminate the ice cream scoops for durability. If desired, create durable ice cream scoops and cones out of foam.

Activity Procedure

1. Review with the students what a pattern is. Remind them that a pattern repeats in a predictable way.
2. Give each student an ice cream cone.
3. Spread the ice cream scoops out in a central location.
4. Have the students create color patterns by placing scoops of ice cream on top of their cones.
5. Have students share their patterns with the other children in the group.

Adaptations

- Allow students to glue the ice cream scoops on the ice cream cone and display the patterns in the classroom.
- Photocopy the ice cream scoops on white cardstock and have the students color the scoops with crayons or markers in order to create their patterns.
- Have students count the number of scoops on each ice cream cone.
- Encourage students to create ice cream cones with varied patterns, such as ABC, AABC, ABBCC, etc. Provide ample scoops of ice cream for this activity.
- Have students guess what comes next in one another's patterns.

Ice Cream Cone Pattern

Ice Cream Scoop Patterns

Edible Jewelry

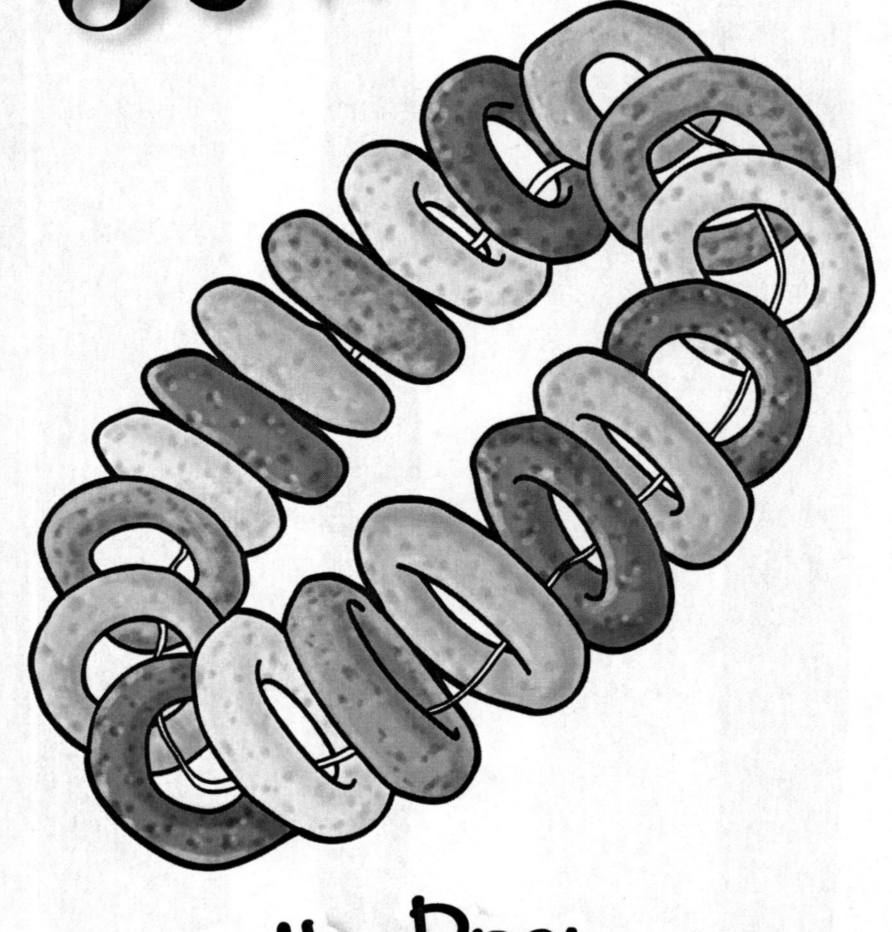

Skill:

Creating patterns

Suggested Group Size:

2–4 students

Activity Overview:

Students create patterned necklaces out of cereal.

Materials:

- string
- scissors
- tape
- colored-O cereal
- paper towels or small bowls

Activity Preparation

1. Cut lengths of string 18" (46.75 cm) long, one per student.
2. Secure tape around one end of each of the strings so that they will not fray as the students are using them.

Activity Procedure

1. Review with the students what a pattern is. Remind them that a pattern repeats in a predictable way.
2. Provide each student with a string and a paper towel or small bowl.
3. Pour some cereal on the paper towel or in the bowl.
4. Tape one end of the string to the table so that the cereal will not slip off the end of the string as students are assembling the necklaces.
5. Have the students use the cereal to form a color pattern by threading the cereal on the string.
6. Tie the ends of the string together to form a circle.
7. Allow students to wear and eat their patterned necklaces.*

Adaptations

- Have students make pattern bracelets.
- Have students make a number pattern with the cereal (i.e. one orange, two green, three pink, etc.).

* Safety Note: Be sure to check for food allergies before having students eat the cereal. Have students remove their necklaces before playing on the playground.

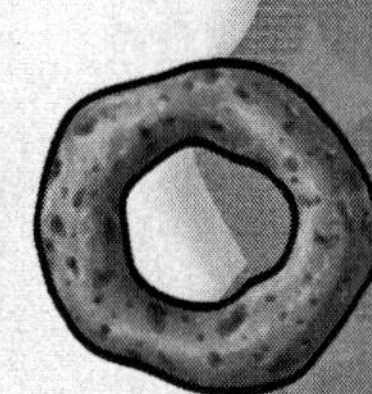

Complete the Clock

Skill:

Identifying numbers

Suggested Group Size:

2–6 students

Activity Overview:

Students match numbers on number cards to the numbers on a clock.

Materials:

- "Clock Pattern" (page 36)
- 1–12 "Number Cards" (pages 169–171)
- crayons or markers

Activity Preparation

1. Photocopy "Clock Pattern," one per student (or print color copies from the CD).
2. Photocopy multiple sets of the number cards on cardstock paper.
3. Cut out the number cards.

Activity Procedure

1. Give each student a clock pattern and crayons or markers.
2. Shuffle the number cards and place them in a central location.
3. Have a student take the top card from the number deck. The student identifies the number and colors the matching number on his or her clock.
4. Have other students take turns following the same procedure. If a number is drawn from the deck that has already been colored on that student's clock, then the student waits until his or her next turn to select another number. The activity is over when all the students have colored all the numbers on the clocks.

Adaptations

- Use dice and change this activity into an addition game. The sum of the two numbers will be the number colored on the clock. (Since the number one cannot be created by the sum of two dice, each student must color the number one prior to starting the activity.)
- To make the game go faster, after the first two rounds, allow students to color the numbers on their clocks each time a card is drawn by any student.
- Include the zero number card. If a student draws the zero card, he or she loses a turn.
- Use the picture of the calculator (page 37) instead of the clock. Use the 0–9 cards.

Clock Pattern

Calculator Pattern

Find Your Partner

Skill:

Identifying numbers

Suggested Group Size:

Whole class

Activity Overview:

Students look for their partners, i.e., pairs of children who have matching numbers.

Materials:

- 1–10 "Number Cards" (pages 169–171)

Activity Preparation

1. Photocopy two sets of the number cards on cardstock paper. Make sure you have one card for each student. (If you have fewer than 20 students, eliminate one or more of the numbers from both sets of cards. If you have more than 20 students, photocopy additional numbers.)
2. Cut out the cards.
3. Laminate the cards for durability.

Activity Procedure

1. Shuffle the cards.
2. Give each student a card.
3. Tell the students they are not allowed to show their cards until everyone has a card.
4. Have the students stand up and walk around the room, looking for the students who have the matching numbers. Once a pair matches up, they can go over to a central location and sit down next to each other.
5. Once all the students have partners, have pairs of students hold up their cards and tell what number is on them.

Adaptations

- Have students match number cards to domino cards (pages 104–105).
- Play a matching game using the shape cards (pages 166–168).
- Have students match numbers to number words (pages 174–176).

Gem Dig

Skill:

Identifying numbers

Suggested Group Size:

2–4 students

Activity Overview:

Students identify numbers as they dig for gems.

Materials:

- "Number Board" (page 42)
- extra large sequins (available at craft stores)
- beach pail or other container
- slotted spoon
- play sand (available at home improvement stores)
- permanent marker

Activity Preparation

1. Photocopy "Number Board" on cardstock paper (or print copies from the CD).
2. Laminate the number board for durability.
3. Write the numbers 1–20 on the sequins, one number per sequin.
4. Fill the pail halfway with the play sand.
5. Place the sequins in the pail.
6. Stir the contents of the pail with the spoon.

Activity Procedure

1. Place the pail, slotted spoon, and number board in the center of the playing area.
2. Have a student use the spoon to dig for a gem. Have him or her read the number on the gem. If the student can identify the number, he or she can place it on the matching number on the number board. If the student cannot identify the number, he or she must return the gem to the pail.
3. Allow other students to take turns, following the same procedure. The activity continues until all the gems have been placed on their corresponding numbers on the number board.

Adaptations

- Photocopy "Number Gems" (pages 43) on cardstock paper. Cut out the paper gems and use in place of the sequins.
- Use beach digging tools.
- Create a number board with addition or subtraction facts. Have students use the gems to show the sum or difference of the problems on the board.
- Write number words on the sequins and have students match the number words to numbers on the number board.
- Place magnetic numbers in the pail instead of the gems.

Number Board

1	2	3	4
5	6	7	8
9	10	11	12
13	14	15	16
17	18	18	20

Number Gems

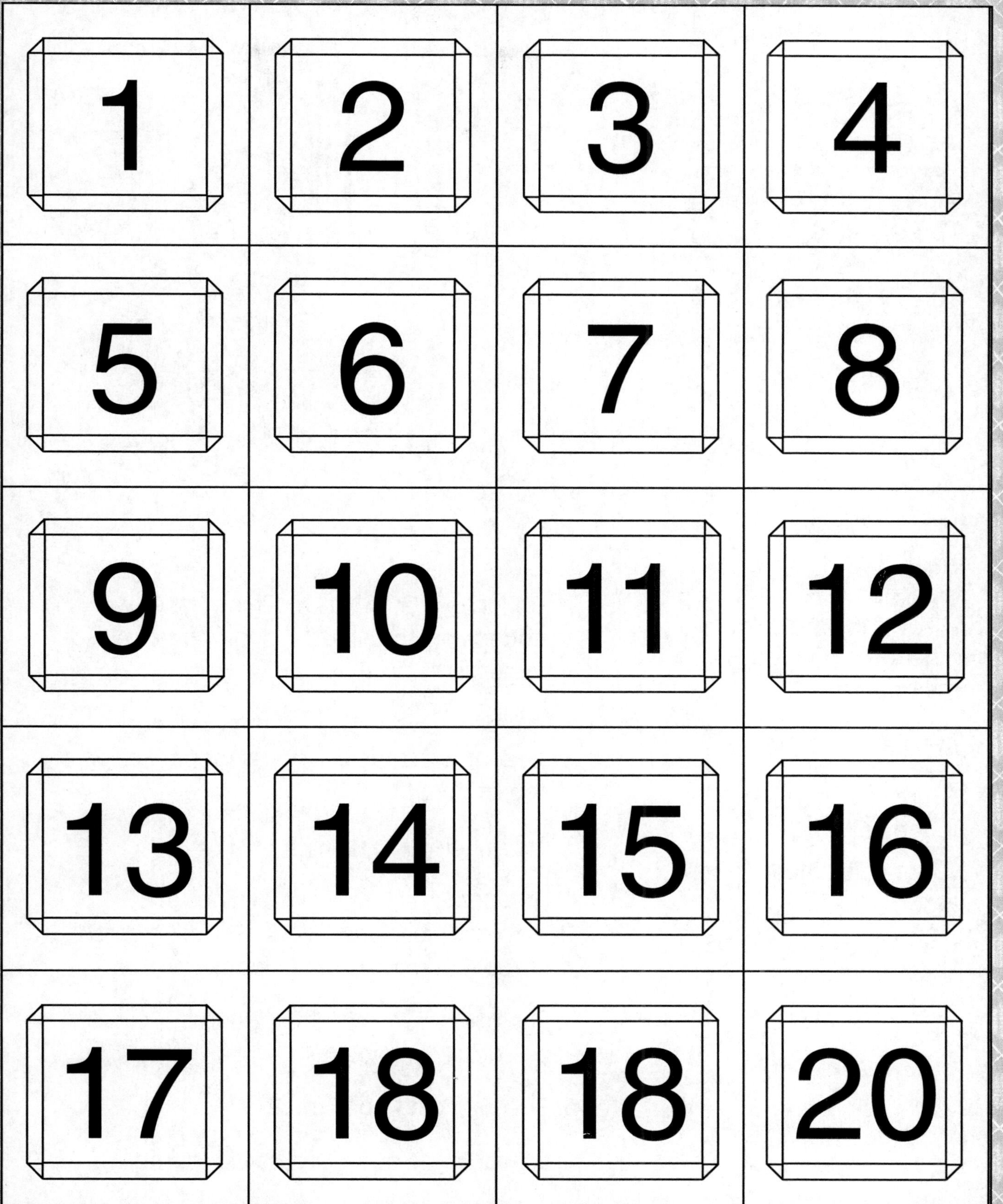

Gum Ball Machine

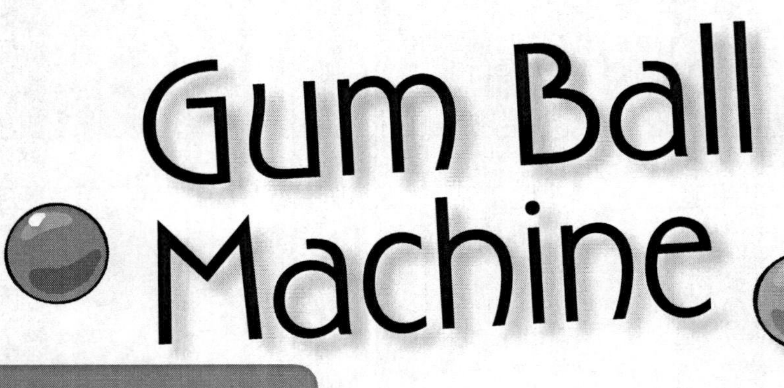

Skill:

Identifying numbers

Suggested Group Size:

2–6 students

Activity Overview:

Students identify numbers on cards and then cover the matching number on a gum ball game mat.

Materials:

- "Gum Ball Machine" (page 46)
- "Gum Ball Patterns" (page 47)
- 0–12 "Number Cards" (pages 168–171)

Activity Preparation

1. Photocopy "Gum Ball Machine," one per student, on cardstock paper (or print color copies from the CD).
2. Photocopy "Gum Ball Patterns," one per student, on cardstock paper (or print color copies from the CD).
3. Cut out the gum balls.
4. Laminate the gum ball machines and gum balls for durability. If desired, create durable gum balls out of foam.
5. Photocopy two sets of 0–12 number cards on cardstock paper.
6. Cut out the number cards.
7. Laminate the number cards for durability.

Activity Procedure

1. Give each student a gum ball machine and 13 gum balls.
2. Shuffle the number cards and place them in a central location.
3. Have a student take the top card from the deck and say the number. If the student correctly identifies the number, he or she can cover the matching number on his or her gum ball machine with a gum ball. If the student cannot identify the number, he or she must wait until his or her next turn to try again. If the student has already covered the number, he or she waits until his or her next turn.
4. Have other students take turns following the same procedure. The game is over when all the students have used all of their gum balls.

Adaptations

- Use two dice to make this game an addition game. Have the students roll both dice and then add the numbers together. The student may use a gum ball to cover the number that is the sum of the dice.
- Use the "Number Words Cards" (pages 174–176). Have students read the number words and cover the corresponding numbers.
- Have the students draw two number cards and find the difference between the numbers.

Gum Ball Machine

Gum Ball Patterns

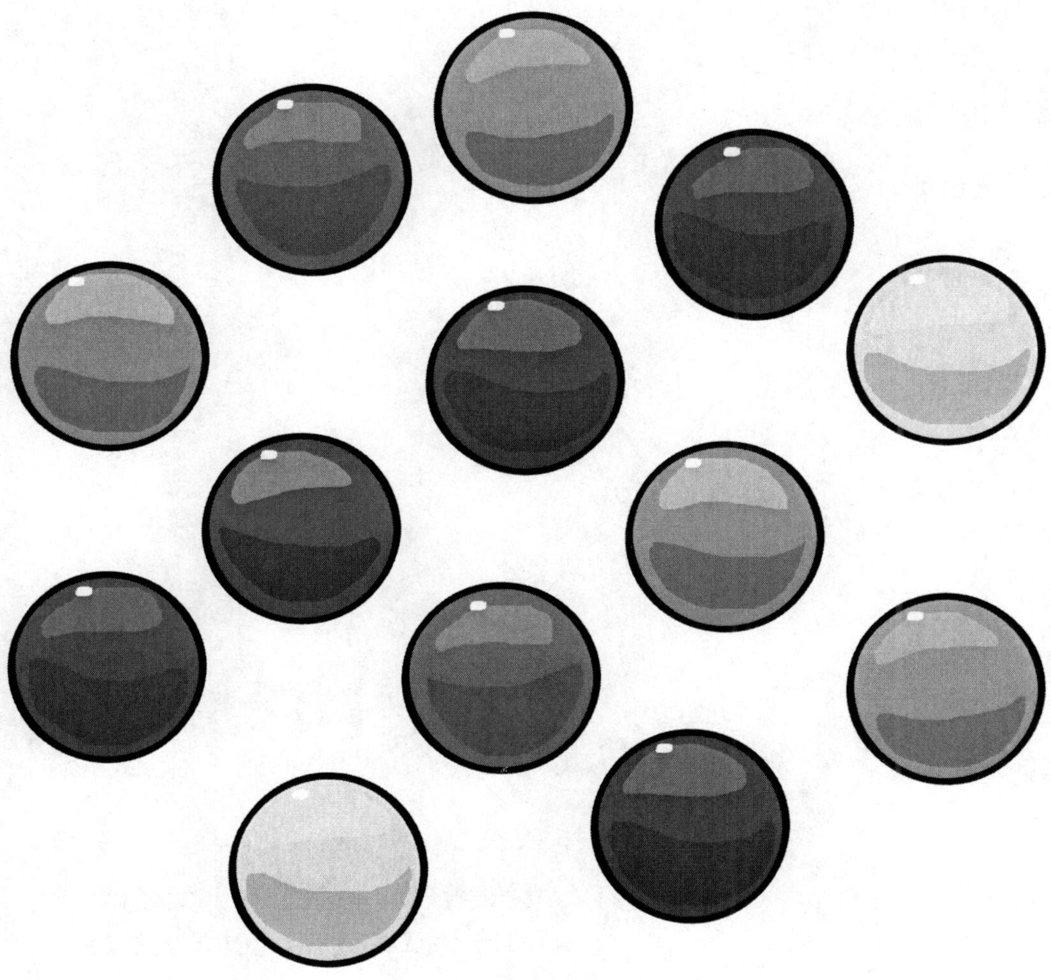

Mail Carrier

Skill:

Identifying numbers

Suggested Group Size:

2–6 students

Activity Overview:

Students match numbers on number cards to numbers on mailboxes.

Materials:

- "Mail Carrier Scene" (page 50)
- 0–6 "Number Cards" (pages 168–170)
- crayons or markers

Activity Preparation

1. Photocopy "Mail Carrier Scene," one for each student (or print color copies from the CD).
2. Photocopy multiple sets of the 0–6 number cards on cardstock paper.

Activity Procedure

1. Give each student "Mail Carrier Scene" and some markers or crayons.
2. Shuffle the number cards and place them in a central location.
3. Have a student take the top card from the number deck. The student colors the mailbox that has the matching number on his or her mail carrier scene.
4. Have other students take turns following the same procedure. If a number is drawn that has already been colored, the student waits until his or her next turn and selects another card. The activity is over when all the numbers have been colored on each student's mail carrier scene.

Adaptations

- Use a die instead of number cards.
- Allow students to draw another card if the number they selected has already been colored on their scenes.
- Use the "Blank Mail Carrier Scene" (page 51). Write numbers that are sums of numbers from 0–6 on the mailboxes. Use multiple sets of the 0–6 cards. Have students take two cards at a time and add the numbers together.
- Draw shapes on the mailboxes on "Blank Mail Carrier Scene." Use "Shape Cards" (pages 166–168) and use the activity for practicing shapes.

Mail Carrier Scene

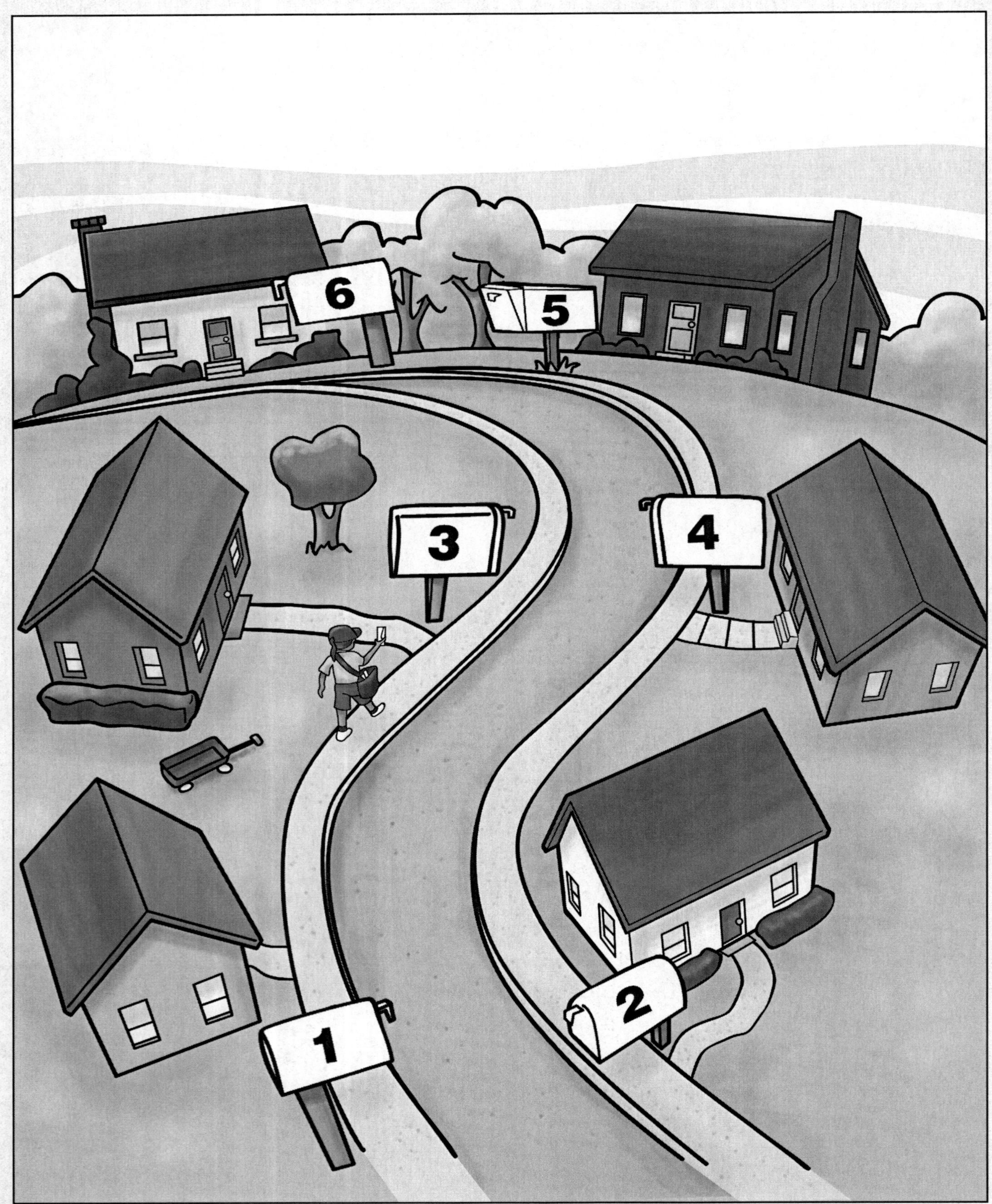

Blank Mail Carrier Scene

Number Match

Skill:

Identifying numbers

Suggested Group Size:

2–6 students

Activity Overview:

Students roll a die and color parts of their pictures that have the same number.

Materials:

- "House Number Match" (page 54)
- a die
- crayons or markers

Activity Preparation

1. Photocopy "House Number Match," one for each student, on regular or cardstock paper (or print copies from the CD).

Activity Procedure

1. Provide each student with "House Number Match" and some crayons or markers.

2. Have a student roll the die.

3. Have the student count the dots on the die and say the number. Then, he or she must find that number on his or her picture. The student then colors that part of the picture according to the color code at the top of the page. (The numbers are in the picture more than one time. The student may only color one space per turn.)

4. Have other students take turns following the same procedure. The activity is over when all the students have colored all the numbers. Allow students to color any unnumbered spaces any color they want.

Adaptations

- Do the activity again using "Flower Number Match" (page 55) as an alternative activity page.
- Use multiple sets of the 1–6 number cards (pages 169–170) instead of a die.
- Disregard the color code. Allow students to color the pictures with colors of their own choosing.
- Use "Beach Number Match" (page 56) or "Farm Number Match" (page 57) to practice larger numbers, or have the students roll two dice and add the numbers together.

House Number Match

1 = red	3 = blue	5 = brown
2 = yellow	4 = green	6 = black

Flower Number Match

1 = green	3 = red	5 = yellow
2 = pink	4 = purple	6 = orange

Beach Number Match

1 = red	4 = yellow	7 = orange	10 = tan
2 = blue	5 = brown	8 = purple	11 = light blue
3 = green	6 = black	9 = pink	12 = lightgreen

Farm Number Match

1 = red	4 = yellow	7 = orange	10 = tan
2 = blue	5 = brown	8 = purple	11 = light blue
3 = green	6 = black	9 = pink	12 = light green

Number Walk

Skill:

Identifying numbers

Suggested Group Size:

Whole class

Activity Overview:

Students walk around numbers written on cards on the floor as music plays. Once the music stops, a number is called and whoever is next to that number counts out loud to that number.

Materials:

- "Number Cards" (pages 168–173)
- radio or CD player/ cassette player
- music (a radio station, CD or tape)

Activity Preparation

1. Photocopy two sets of "Number Cards" on cardstock paper.
2. Cut out the cards.
3. Laminate the cards for durability.

Activity Procedure

1. Place one set of cards faceup on the floor in a circle, leaving about two feet between each card.
2. Have each student stand next to a different card.
3. Remove any extra cards from the floor. Remove the same numbers from the other set of cards. This is the set you will be using.
4. Play music and instruct students to walk counterclockwise.
5. Stop the music at various intervals. When you stop the music, have the students stop walking and stand next to a number card.
6. Take the top card from your deck and hold up the card.
7. Have all the students say the name of the number. Have the student standing next to that number count out loud up to that number.
8. Continue playing until all the numbers have been called.

Adaptations

- Have students hop or take baby steps instead of walking while the music plays.
- Instead of having students count up to the number shown, have them jump, clap, or touch their toes that many times.
- Draw dots on pieces of paper that correspond to the numbers on the number cards. Place the papers with the dots on the ground in a circle. Play the game in the same manner as described above. When the music stops, students must count the dots on their papers in order to identify the number next to which they are standing.

Short Racers

Skill:

Identifying numbers

Suggested Group Size:

2–6 students

Activity Overview:

Students race cars by rolling a die and moving their race cars to the matching numbers on their short tracks.

Materials:

- "Short Racer Game Mat" (pages 62–63)
- die
- toy cars or other space markers

Activity Preparation

1. Photocopy "Short Racer Game Mat," one per student (or print color copies from the CD).
2. Cut out and assemble the game boards on the glue tabs to create one large game mat per student.
3. Laminate the game boards for durability.

Activity Procedure

1. Give each student a game mat and three toy cars or other space markers.
2. Have a student roll the die and move his or her car to the matching number on any of his or her racetracks. Cars may only move one space at a time, so if the number rolled is not the very first or next number on a track, the car remains still.
3. Have other students take turns following the same procedure. The game continues until each student has a race car winner.

Adaptations

- Use 1–6 number cards (pages 169–170) instead of a die.
- Have two students share a game mat.
- Create your own game board using "Blank Short Racer Game Mat" (pages 64–65). Fill in the spaces on the game board prior to photocopying. Practice other math skills such as shape identification, addition or subtraction.

Short Racer Game Mat

START

1	2	3	4
3	4	5	6
6	5	4	3

FINISH

4	5	3	2
3	1	2	6
1	6	4	1

GLUE TAB

Short Racer Game Mat (cont.)

Blank Short Racer Game Mat

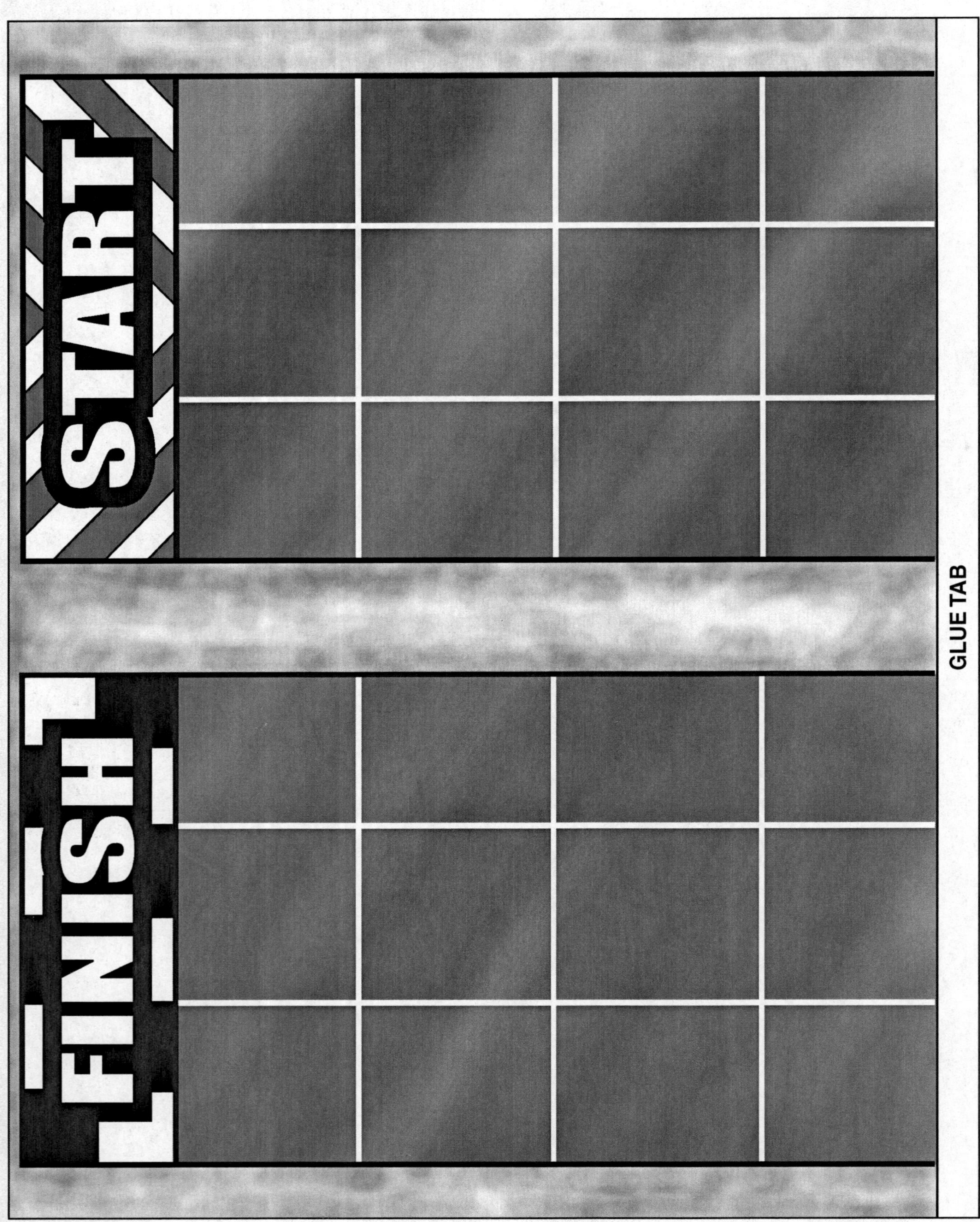

Blank Short Racer Game Mat (cont.)

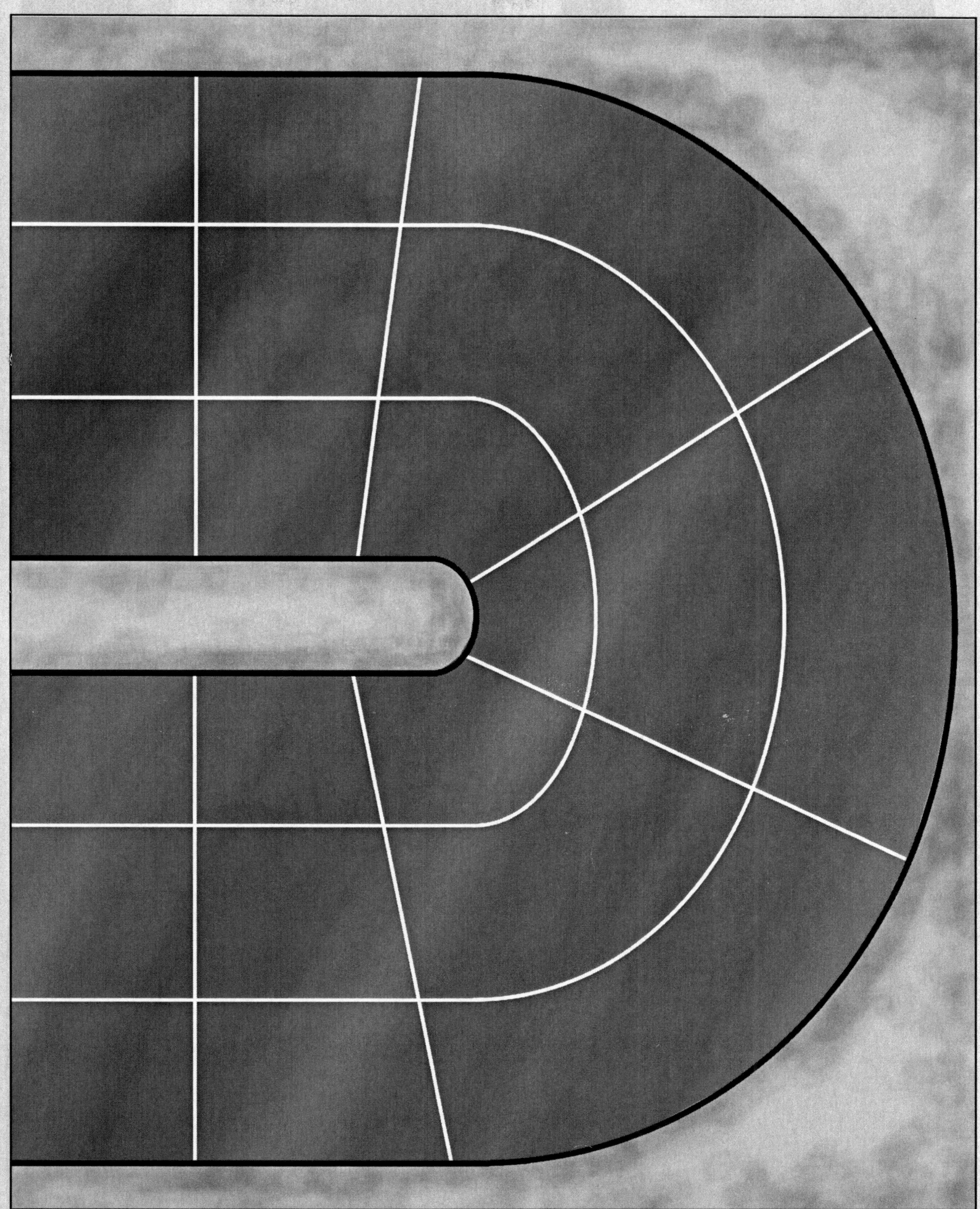

Winner Takes All

Skill:

Identifying numbers

Suggested Group Size:

2–6 students

Activity Overview:

Students collect number cards based on the highest number shown.

Materials:

- 0–20 "Number Cards" (pages 168–173)

Activity Preparation

1. Photocopy multiple sets of 0–20 "Number Cards."
2. Cut out the number cards.
3. Laminate the number cards for durability.

Activity Procedure

1. Place the shuffled cards facedown in a central location.
2. Have each student take one card off the deck.
3. Have the students show their cards and say what numbers they have. The student with the highest number takes all of the cards for that round.
4. Continue play until all the cards have been used.

Adaptations

- Instead of the highest number winning, have the student with the lowest number take all the cards.
- Change this game into an addition or subtraction game. Each player takes two cards from the deck. The one with the highest sum or greatest difference wins that round.
- Instead of students taking the cards of others after winning a hand, allow students to keep their cards.
- Use only the 0–10 number cards.

Skill:

Counting

Suggested Group Size:

Whole class

Activity Overview:

Students count as they perform various actions.

Materials:

- "Action Cards" (pages 70–73)
- 0–20 "Number Cards" (pages 168–173)

Activity Preparation

1. Photocopy "Action Cards" on cardstock paper (or print color copies from the CD).
2. Cut out the action cards.
3. Photocopy "Number Cards" on cardstock paper.
4. Cut out the number cards.
5. Laminate the number cards and action cards for durability.

Activity Procedure

1. Shuffle the number cards and place them facedown in a pile in a central location. Place the the action cards facedown in a pile next to the number cards.

2. Have a student take the card off the top of the number card deck. Have that same student take the top card off the action pile. The student then shows both cards to the group and performs the action the specified number of times.

3. Have other students take turns following the same procedure. The activity is over when all the cards have been used.

Adaptations

- Once the student performs the action, have him or her lead the group in performing the same action.
- Have the student keep the number a secret, and have other students count as the student performs the required action.
- Use blank index cards to record other actions that students brainstorm.
- Use a die instead of number cards.

Action Cards

jump

clap

Action Cards (cont.)

touch
toes

pat
head

roll over

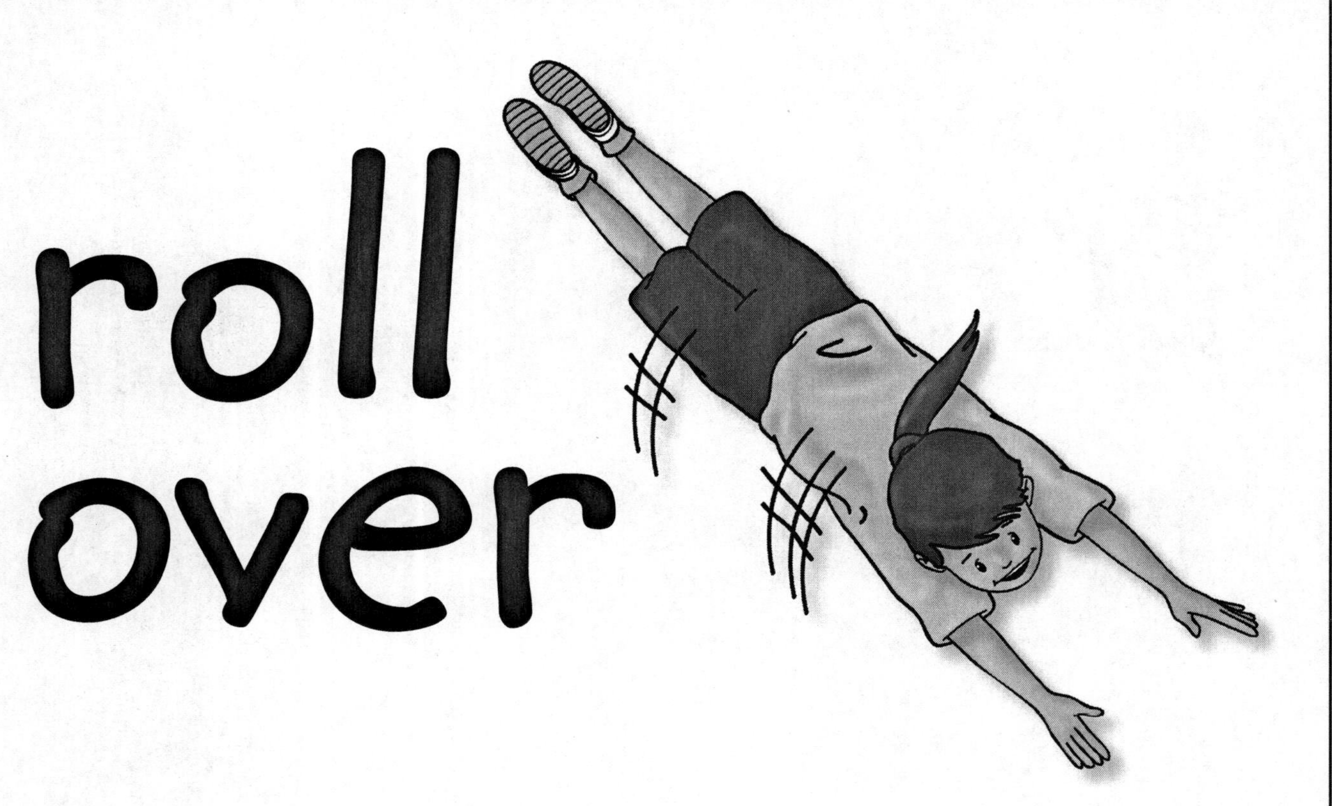

walk on toes

stomp
feet

turn
around

Apple Picking

Skill:

Counting

Suggested Group Size:

2–6 students

Activity Overview:

Students count apples as determined by a roll of a die.

Materials:

- "Apple Tree" (pages 76–77)
- "Basket Pattern" (page 78)
- "Apple Patterns" (page 79) or beans to represent apples
- die

Activity Preparation

1. Photocopy "Apple Tree" on cardstock paper (or print color copies from the CD).
2. Cut out the apple tree, and glue the pages together on the glue tab to create one large playing mat. Laminate the apple tree for durability.
3. Photocopy "Basket Pattern," one per student, on cardstock paper, and color as desired (or print color copies from the CD).
4. Cut out the baskets.
5. Photocopy several copies of "Apple Patterns" on card stock paper, and color as desired (or print color copies from the CD) or gather beans to use instead of the apple patterns. (You may wish to spray paint the beans red so they look more like apples.)

Activity Procedure

1. Provide each student with a basket.
2. Place the apple tree in a central location.
3. Determine the total number of apples to use by the amount of time you want the game to last. (More apples will require more playing time.)
4. Place the apples on the apple tree.
5. Have a student roll the die. The student counts the number of dots on the die, takes the same number of apples off the tree, and places them in his or her basket.
6. Have other students take turns following the same procedure. The activity is over when all the apples have been placed in the baskets. A student needs to roll the exact number in order to take the final apples off the tree.

Adaptations

- Use number cards (pages 168–173) instead of a die. Photocopy multiple sets of the cards to ensure having enough cards when playing the game.
- Have students add the numbers of two dice together. The sum will be the number of apples the student takes off the tree.

Apple Tree

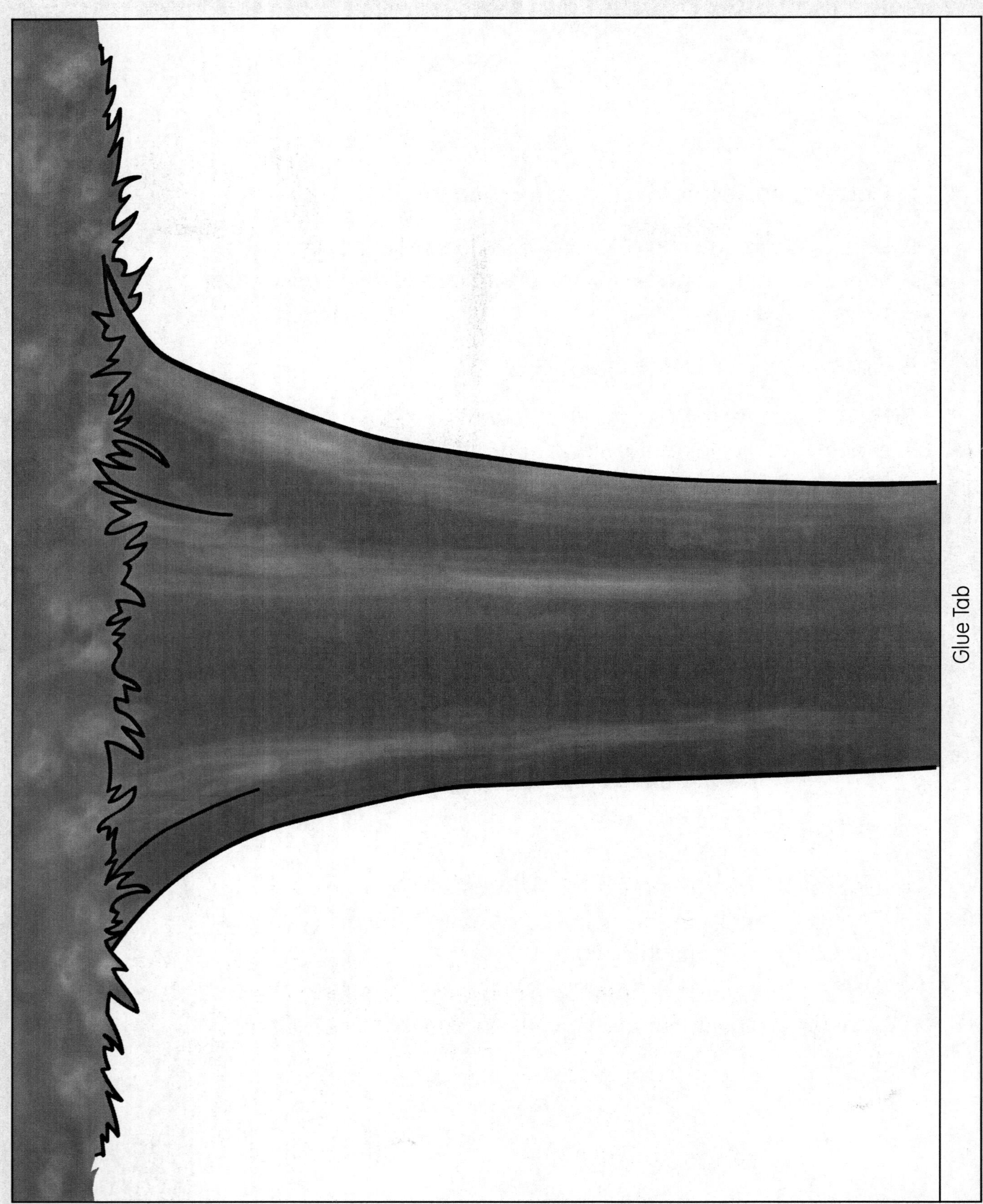

Apple Tree (cont.)

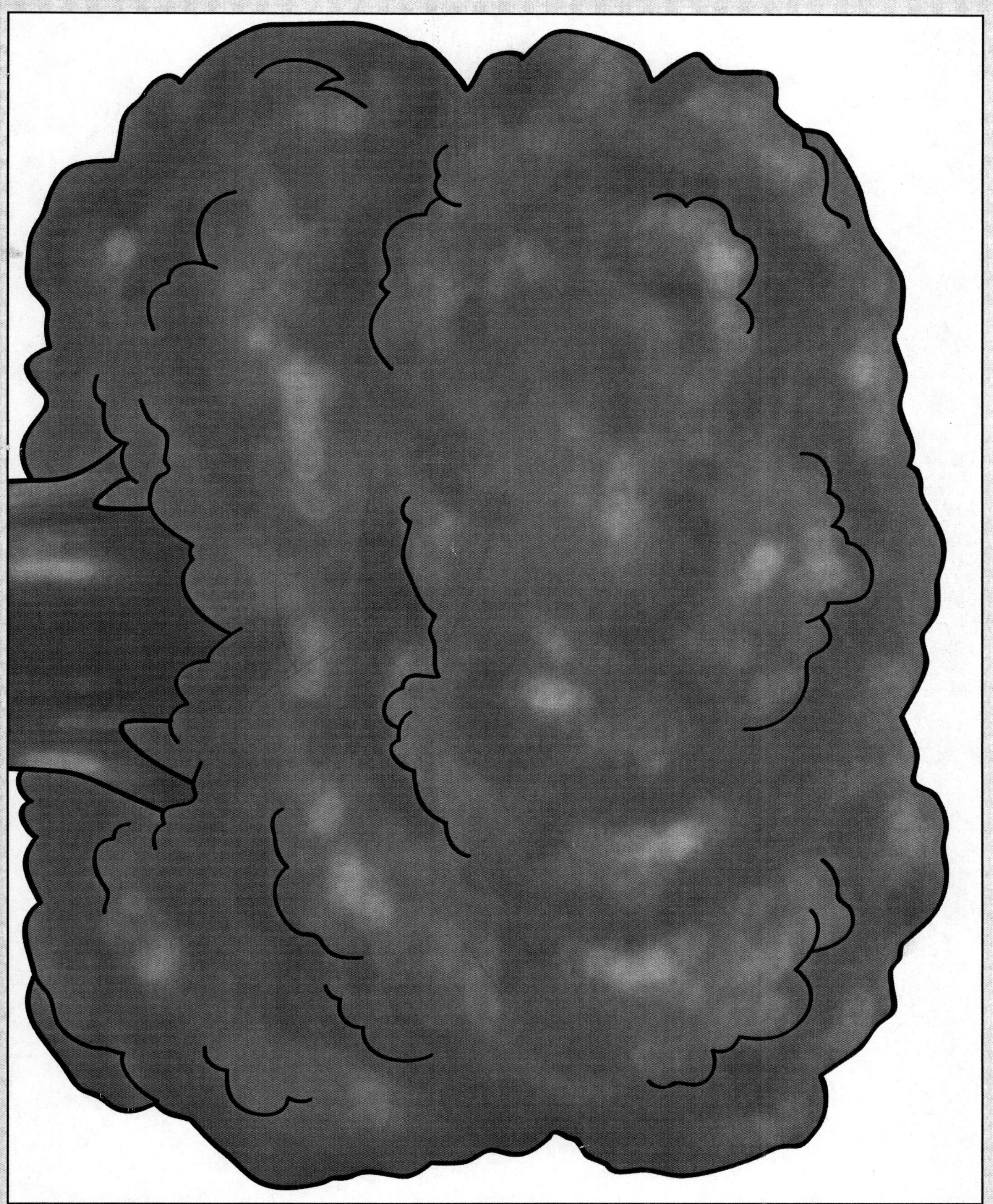

Apple Basket

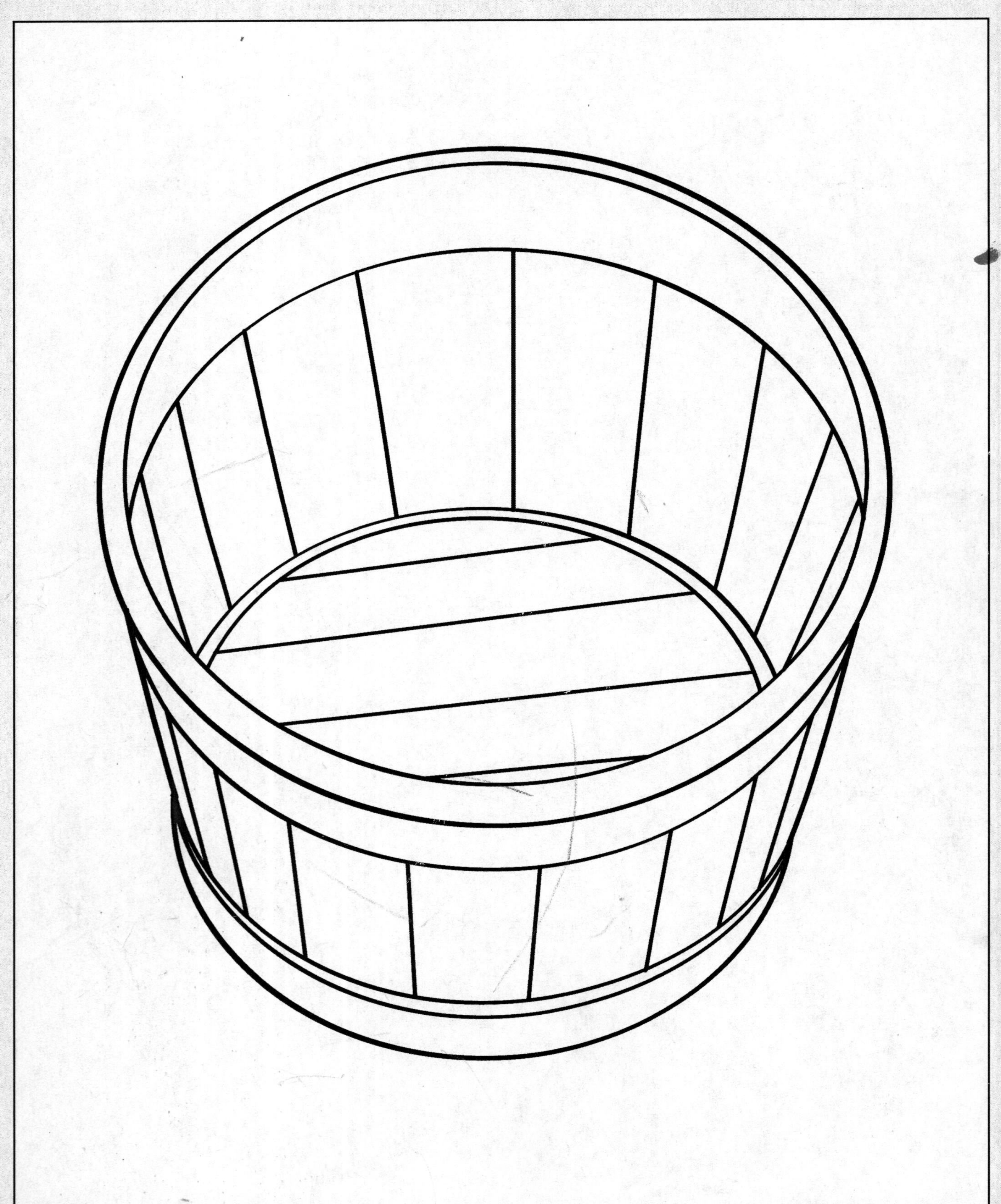

Activity Procedure

1. Give each student the giraffe picture and some markers or crayons.
2. Have a student roll the die. The student colors the same number of spots on his or her giraffe as the number rolled.
3. Have other students take turns following the same procedure. The activity is over when all the giraffes have all of the spots colored. When only a few spots remain, the exact number needed must be rolled in order to finish coloring the spots.

Adaptations

- Use two dice and have students find the difference of the numbers rolled. Color the same number of spots as the difference between the two numbers rolled.
- Use multiple sets of the 0–6 number cards at the back of this book instead of dice.
- Photocopy "Leopard Family" (page 83) and follow the same procedure.

Giraffe Pattern

Leopard Family

Cookie Numbers

Skill:

Counting

Suggested Group Size:

2–6 students

Activity Overview:

Students review numbers and counting as they remove numbered cookies from a cookie sheet.

Materials:

- "Cookie Patterns" (pages 86–89)
- cookie sheet
- spatula
- paper plates

Activity Preparation

1. Photocopy "Cookie Patterns" on cardstock paper (or print color copies from the CD).
2. Cut out the cookies.
3. Write the corresponding number on the back of each card so the number of chocolate chips on the front matches the number written on the back.
4. Laminate the cookies for durability. If desired, create durable cookie pieces out of foam.

Activity Procedure

1. Place the cookies, chocolate chip side up, on the cookie sheet.
2. Place the cookie sheet in the center of the playing area.
3. Give each child a paper plate.
4. Have a student use the spatula to take a cookie off the cookie sheet.
5. Have the student count the number of chocolate chips on the cookie. The cookie can be turned over to check the answer. If the student is correct, he or she may place the cookie on the paper plate. If the student is not correct, he or she places the cookie back on the cookie sheet.
6. Have other students take turns following the same procedure. The activity is over when all the cookies have been placed onto plates. Then students may count the chocolate chips again as the cookies are placed back onto the cookie sheet.

Adaptations

- Continue the game by having students place the cookies back onto the cookie sheet.
- Create a poster displaying the same numbers as are used in the game. Have students match the cookies to the numbers on the poster. The shape of the poster could be a giant cookie sheet.
- Have the students draw their own chocolate chip cookies. Have them write the corresponding numbers on the backs of the cookies.

Cookie Patterns

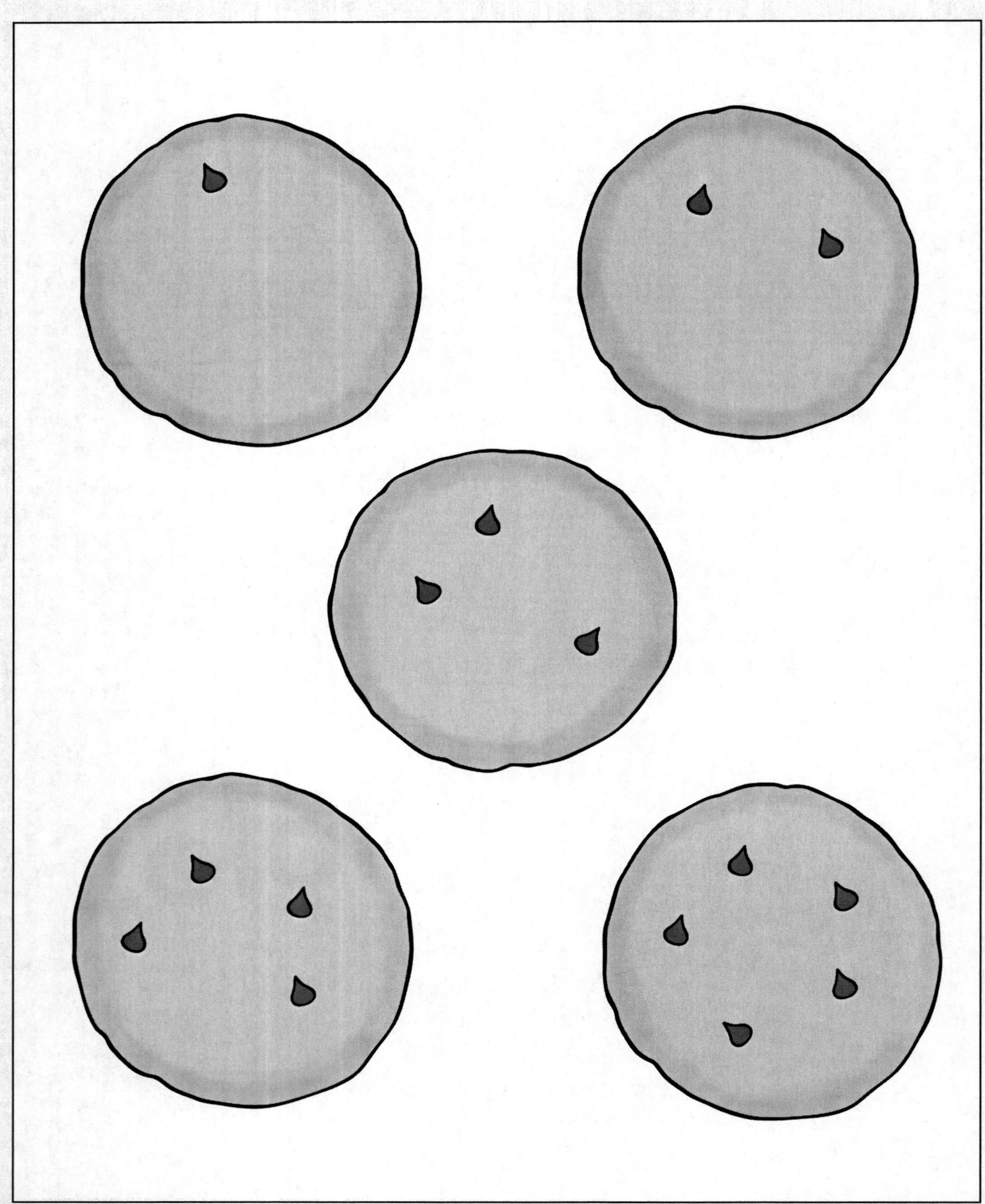

Cookie Patterns (cont.)

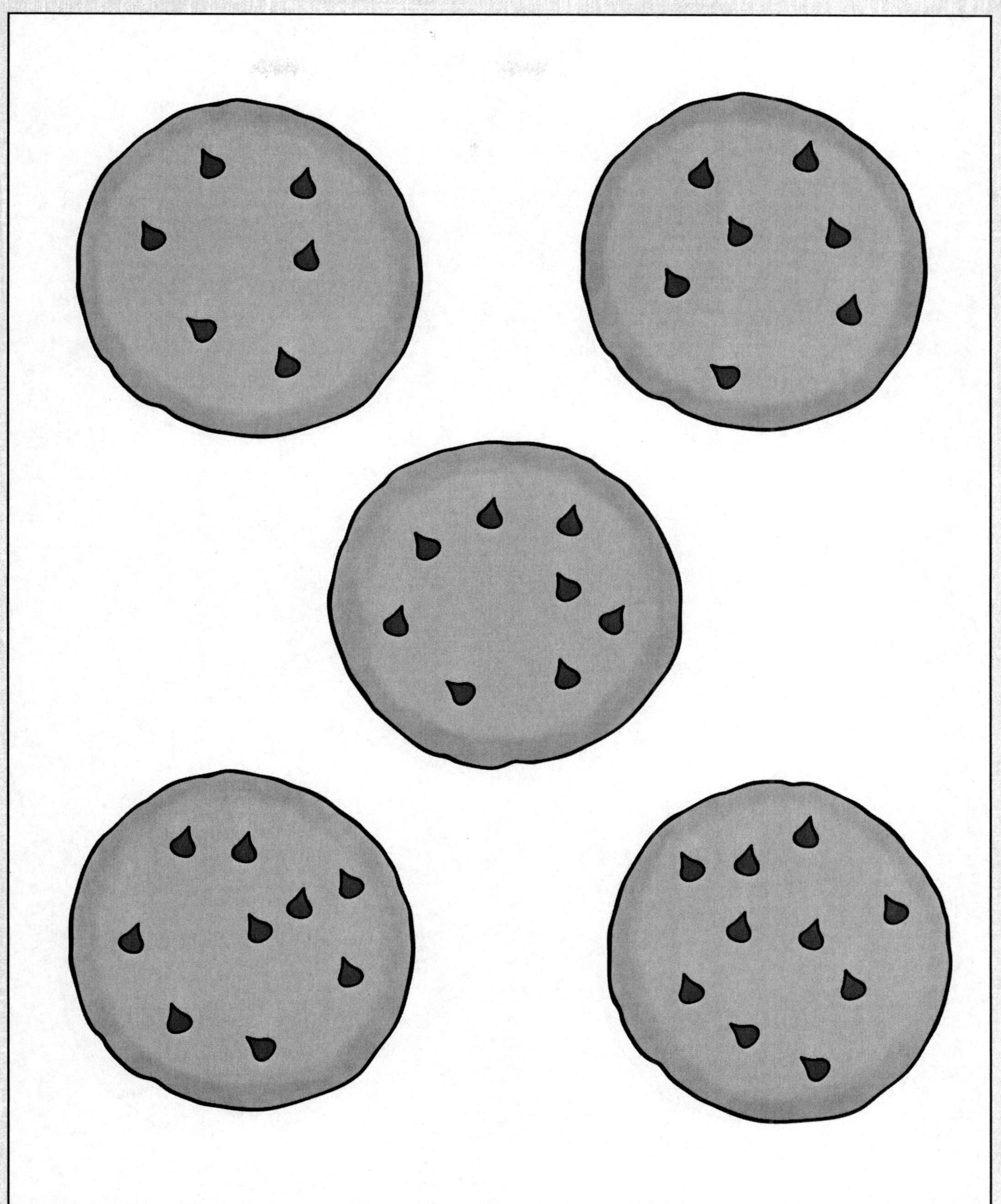

Cookie Patterns (cont.)

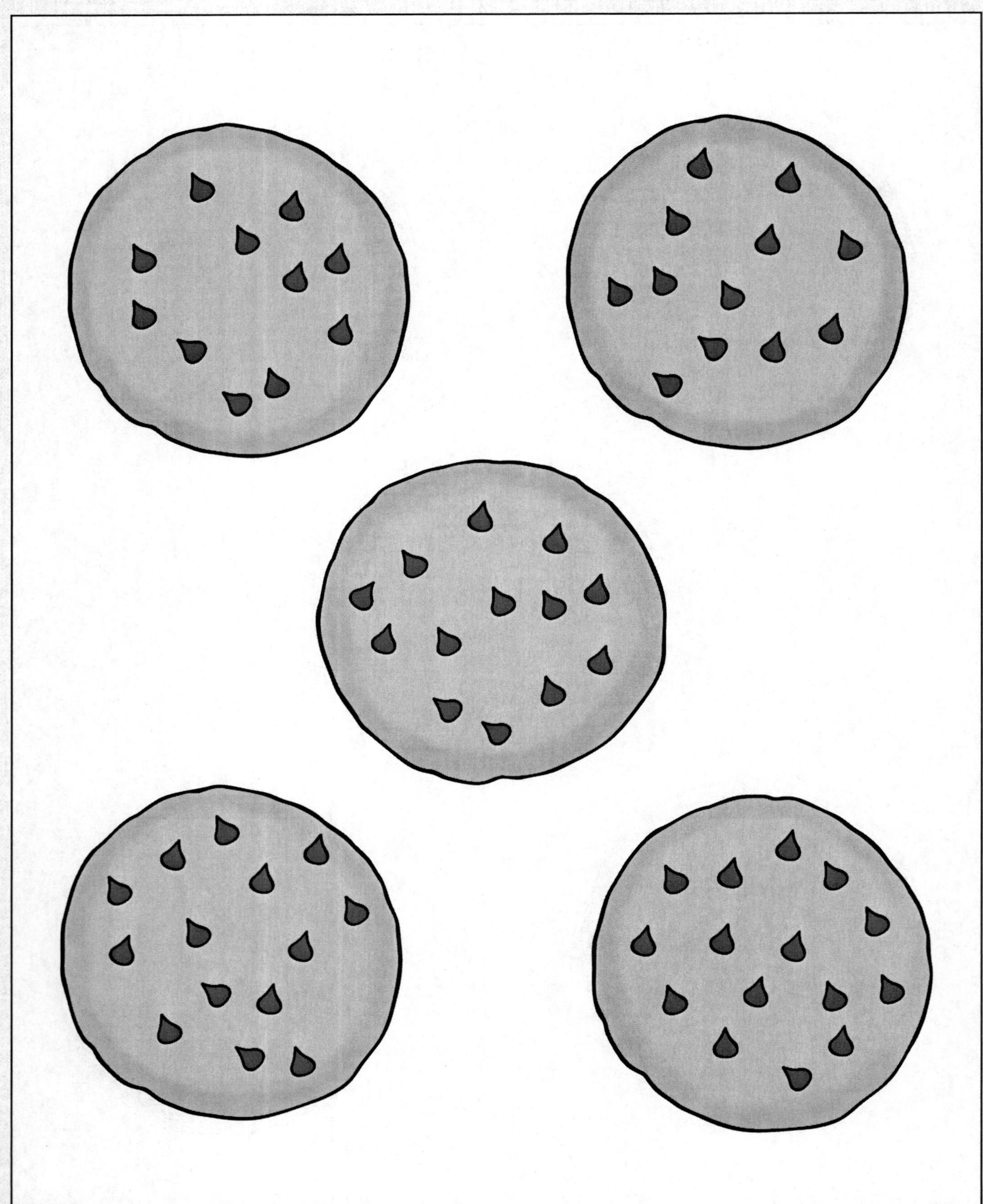

Cookie Patterns (cont.)

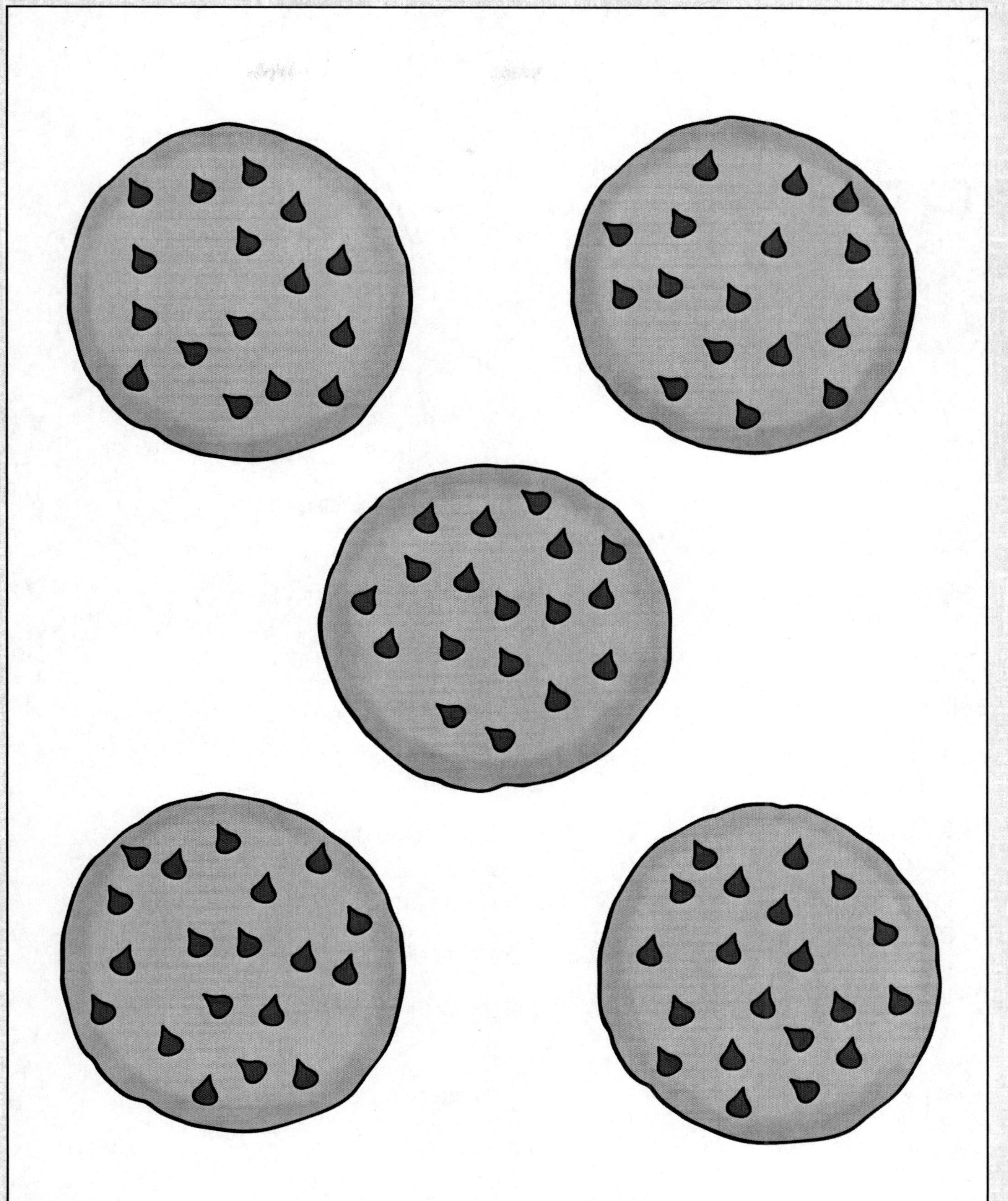

Skill:

Counting

Suggested Group Size:

2–3 students

Activity Overview:

Students match numbers to dots on dog bones.

Materials:

- "Dog Bone Game Mat" (page 92)
- "Dog Bone Patterns" (page 93)
- 1–12 "Number Cards" (pages 169–171)
- dog bowl (optional)

Activity Preparation

1. Photocopy "Dog Bone Game Mat," one per student, on cardstock paper (or print color copies from the CD).
2. Photocopy "Dog Bone Patterns," one per student, on cardstock paper (or print color copies from the CD).
3. Cut out the dog bones.
4. Photocopy three sets of 1–12 "Number Cards."
5. Cut out the number cards.
6. Laminate the game mats, dog bones, and number cards for durability.

Activity Procedure

1. Give each student a game mat. Place dog bones in a central location, or in the dog bowl.
2. Shuffle the number cards and place them facedown.
3. Have a student take a card from the deck. The student says the number on the card and finds a bone with the corresponding number of dots on it on his or her mat. The student then takes a bone from the dog bone pile and matches it to the dotted bone on the game mat. If the student has already covered up that bone, he or she returns the number card to the bottom of the deck and waits until his or her next turn.
4. Continue to show the cards, following the same procedure. The game is over when all the students have covered all the dotted bones on their game mats.

Adaptations

- Have students count to the number shown for each card.
- Instead of using the 1–12 number cards, use dice. Change this activity into an addition challenge. Have the students roll the dice, add numbers on the two dice, and cover the matching dog bones on their mats. (Students must cover the number one space before beginning the activity.)
- Add a subtraction component to this activity. Have students roll a die and remove the corresponding number of dog bones from their mats at the end of the game.
- Have students use real dog biscuits to cover the bones on their game mats.

Dog Bone Game Mat

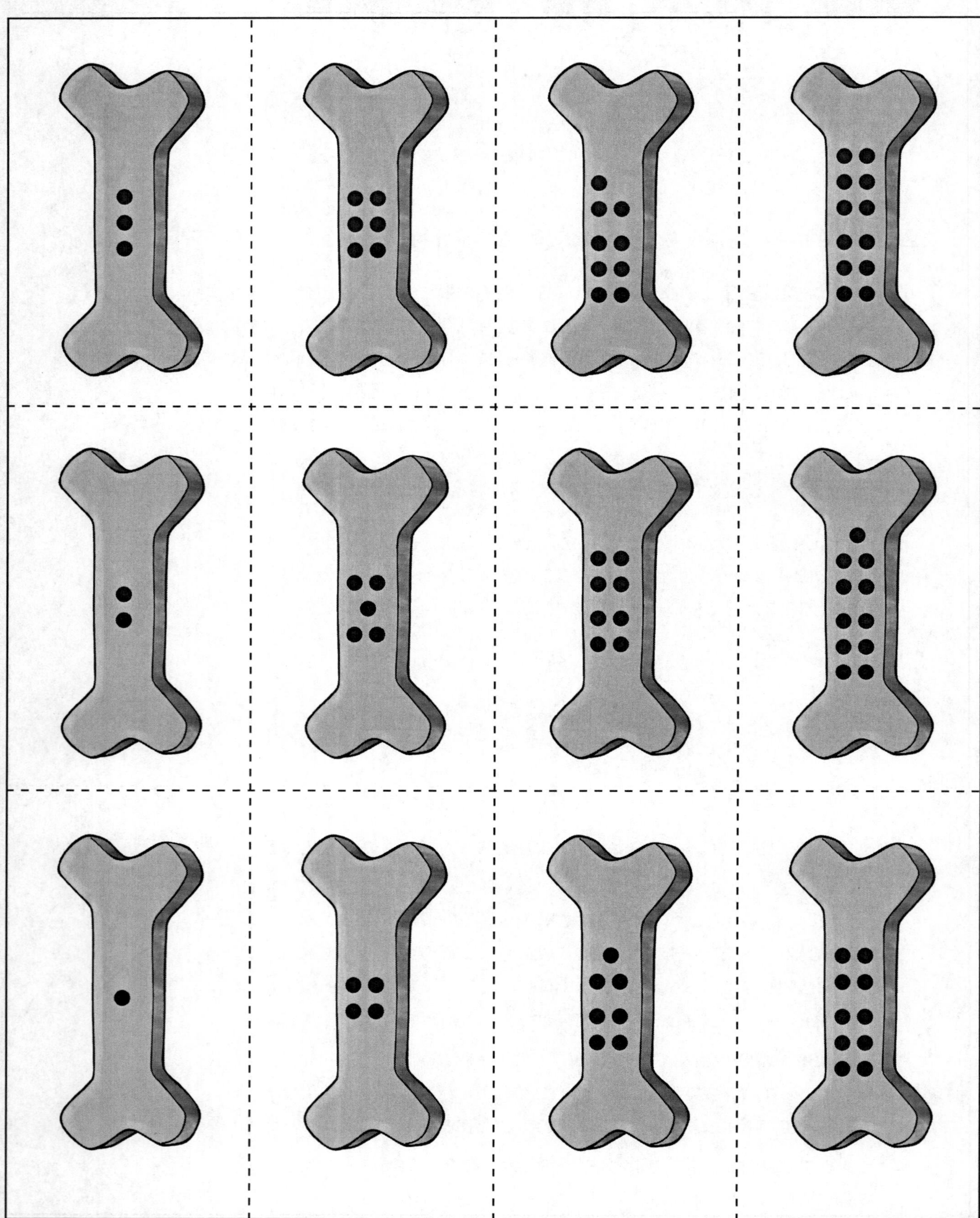

Dog Bone Patterns

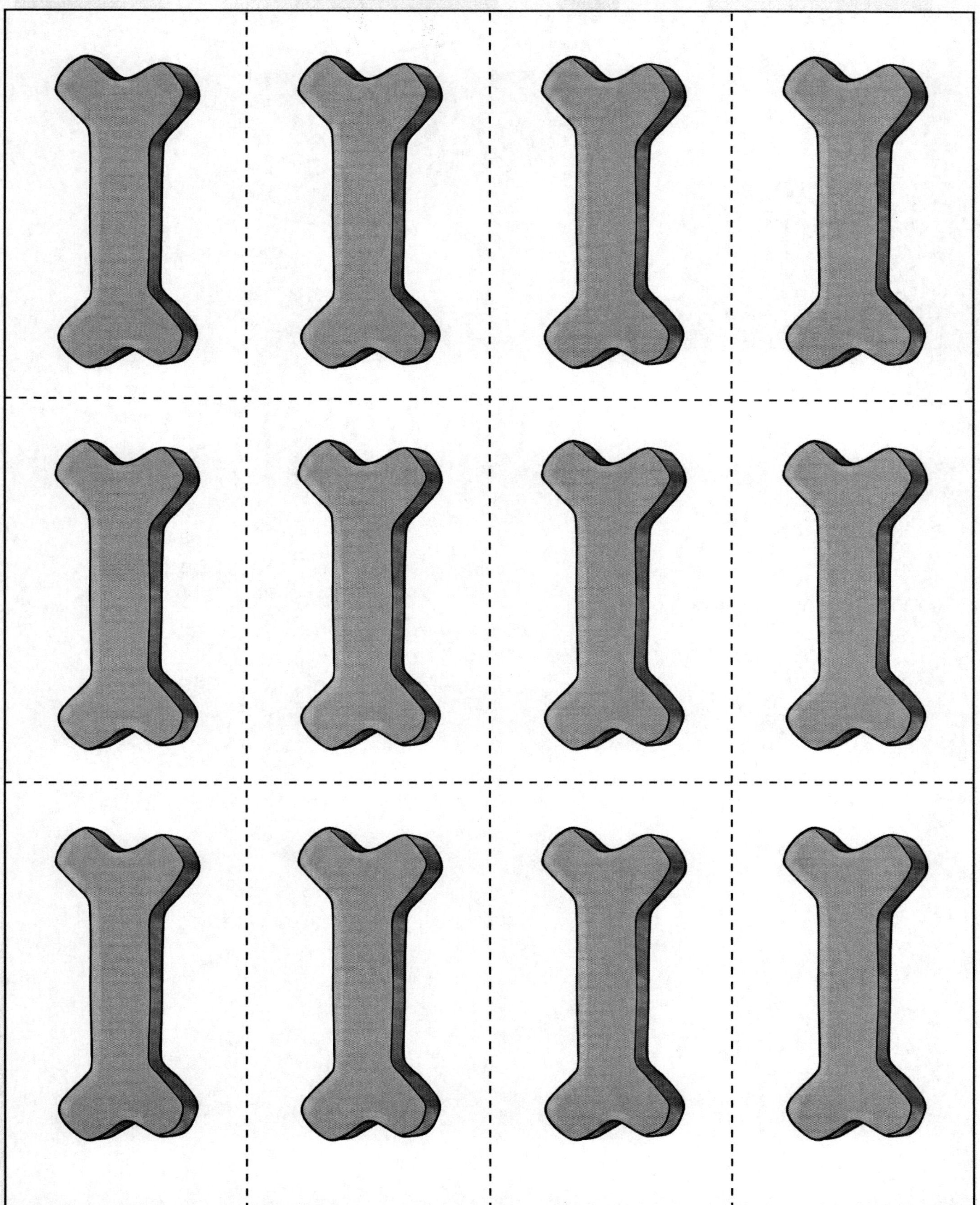

Feed the Monkey

Skill:

Counting

Suggested Group Size:

2–6 students

Activity Overview:

Students "feed" bananas to a monkey according to the number they roll on a die.

Materials:

- "Monkey Pattern" (pages 96–97)
- "Banana Patterns" (page 98)

Activity Preparation

1. Photocopy "Monkey Pattern," on cardstock paper, and color as desired (or print color copies from the CD).
2. Cut out the pieces along the lines and cut out the monkey's mouth.
3. Place glue along the glue tab and assemble the two monkey pieces to create one large monkey.
4. Photocopy six copies of "Banana Patterns" on cardstock paper (or print color copies from the CD).
5. Cut out the bananas.
6. Laminate the monkey and bananas for durability.

Activity Procedure

1. Place the monkey and bananas in a central location.
2. Have a student roll the die. He or she then counts out the corresponding number of bananas. If the student counts the bananas correctly, he or she can put the bananas in the monkey's mouth. If the student does not count the bananas correctly, he or she must return the bananas to the pile.
3. Have other students take turns following the same procedure. The game is over when all the bananas are gone.

Adaptations

- Photocopy and use multiple sets of the 0–6 number cards at the back of this book instead of the die.
- Use dice and have students add the two numbers together. The student then will feed the monkey the number of bananas indicated by the total of the dice.
- Create a bunny and have students feed the bunny carrots (pages 99–101).

Monkey Pattern

Monkey Pattern (cont.)

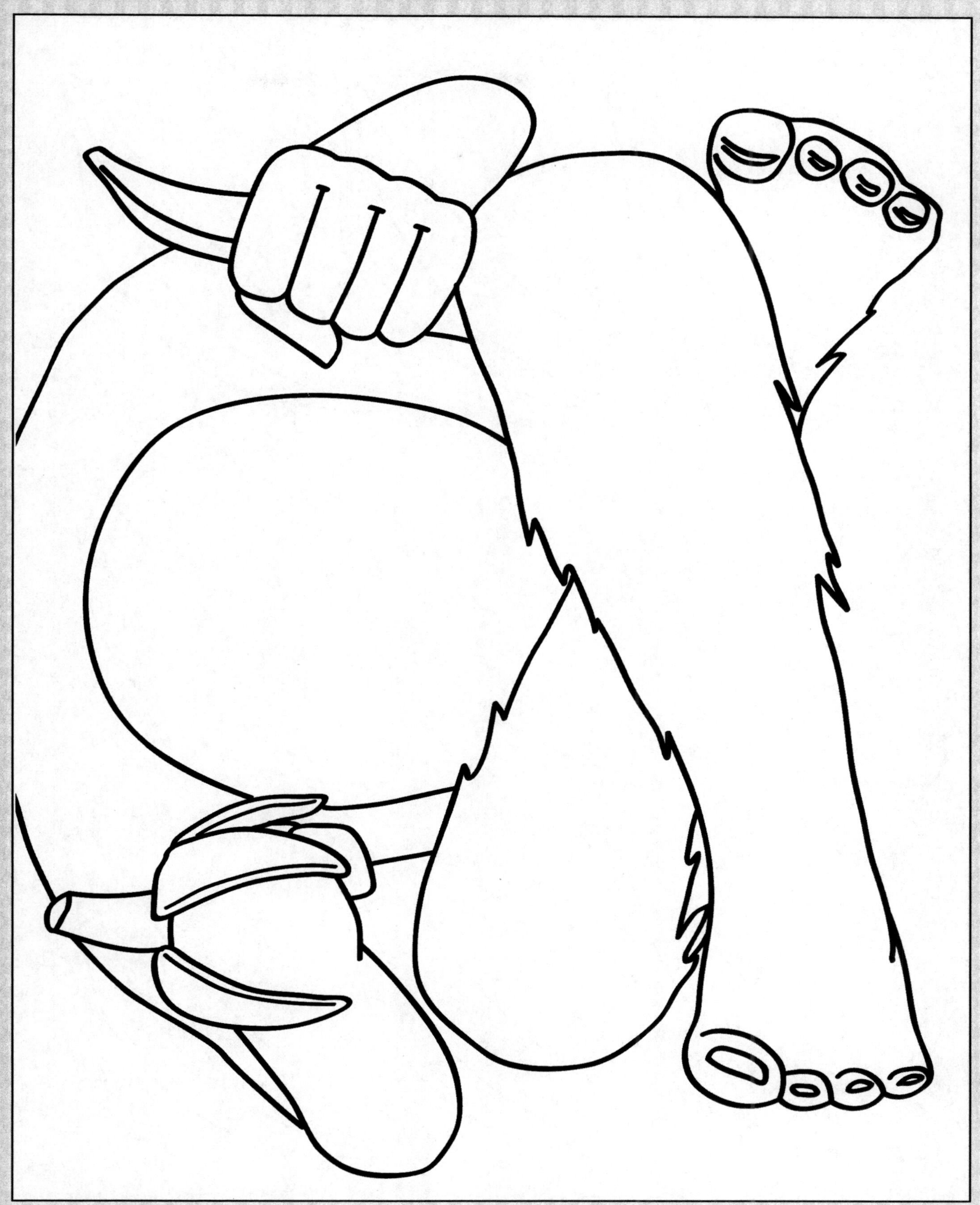

Banana Patterns

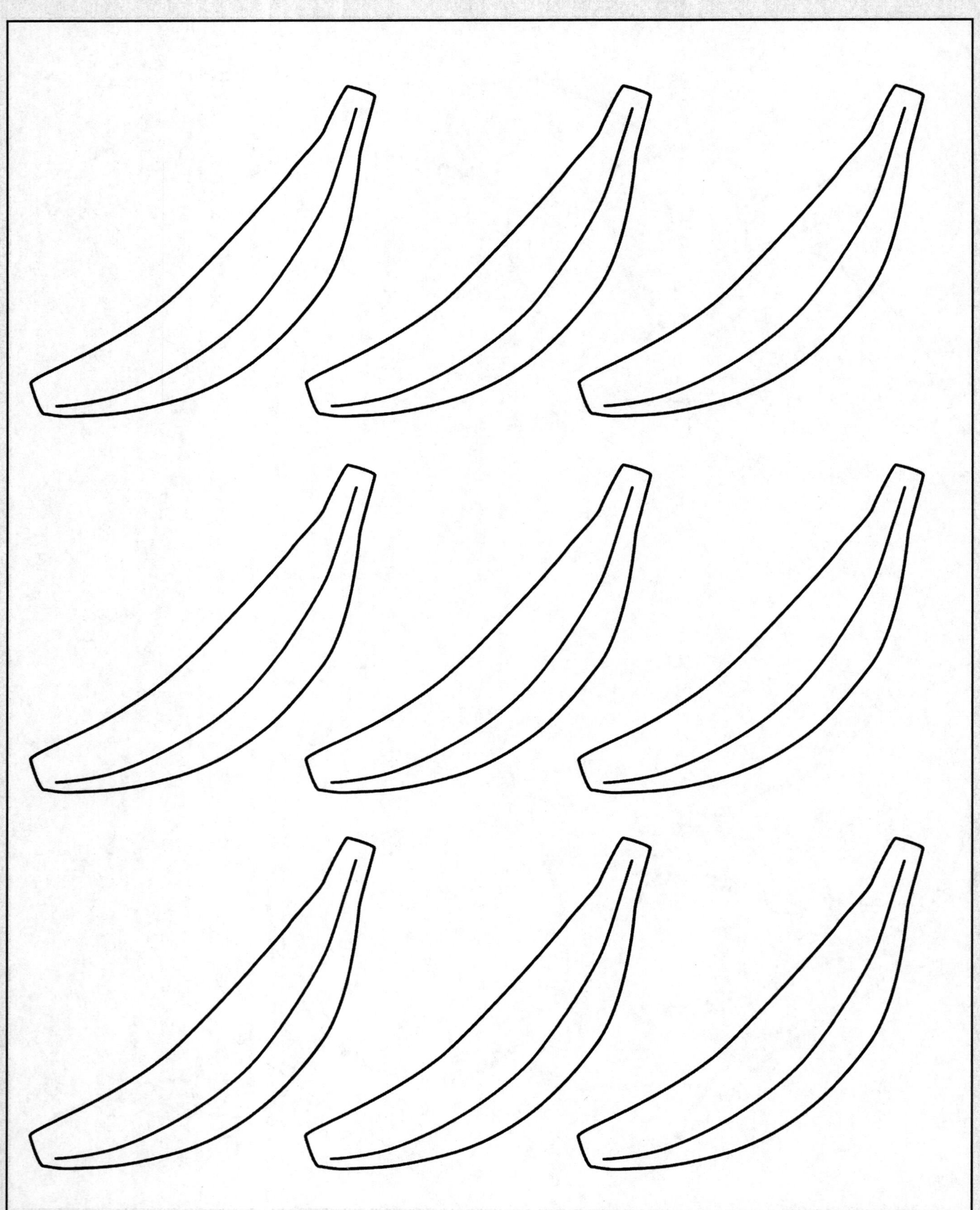

Carrot Patterns

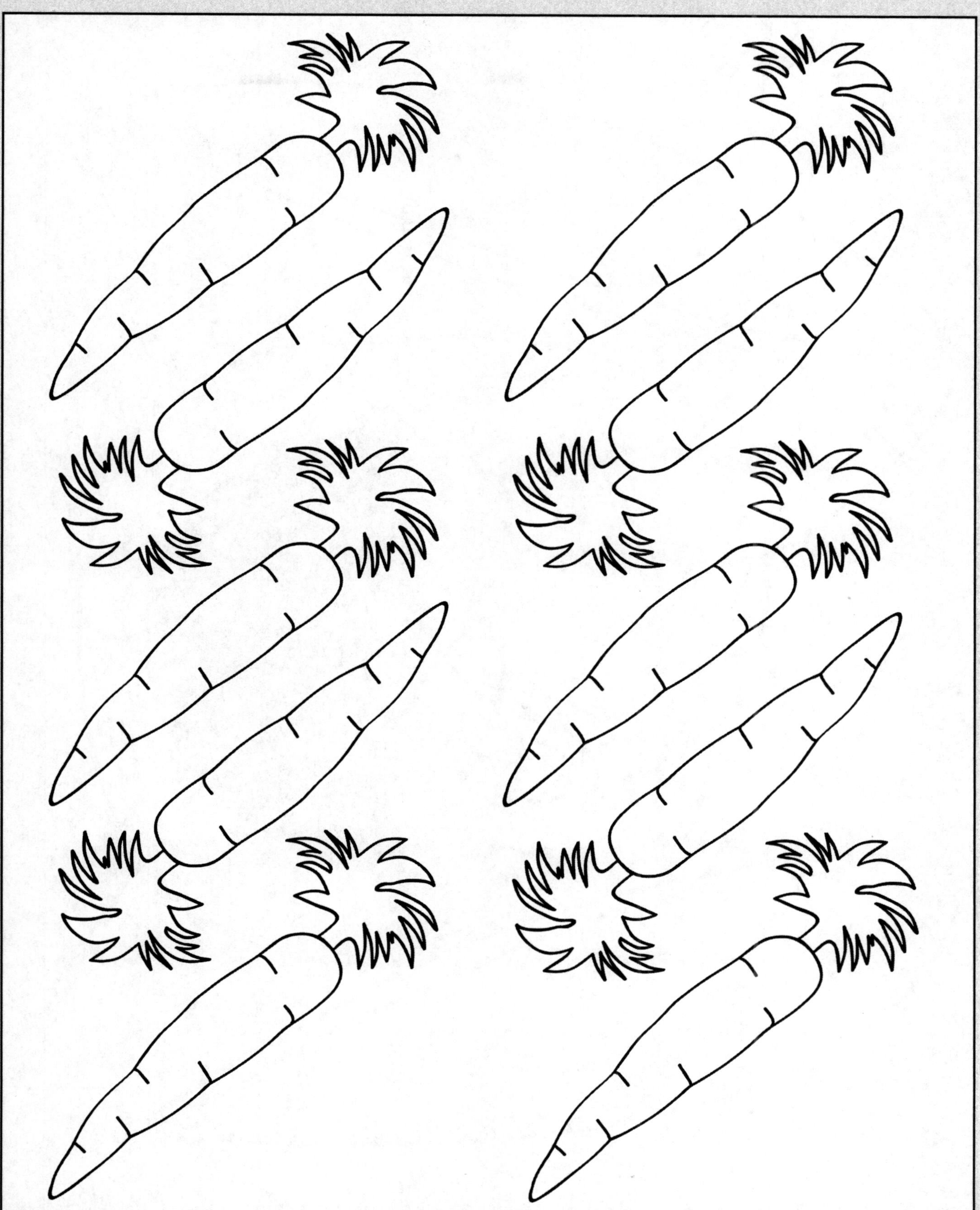

Bunny Pattern

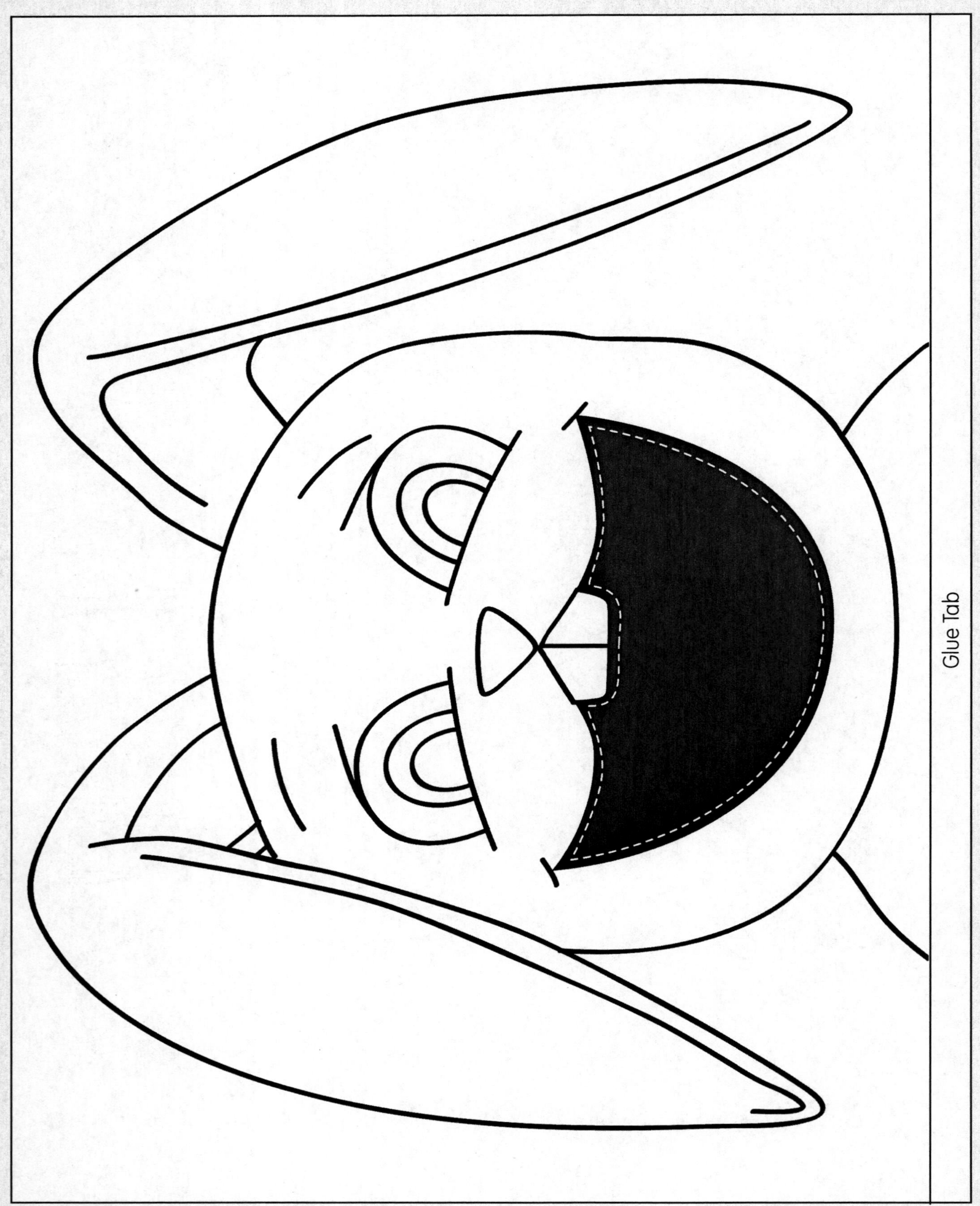

Bunny Pattern (cont.)

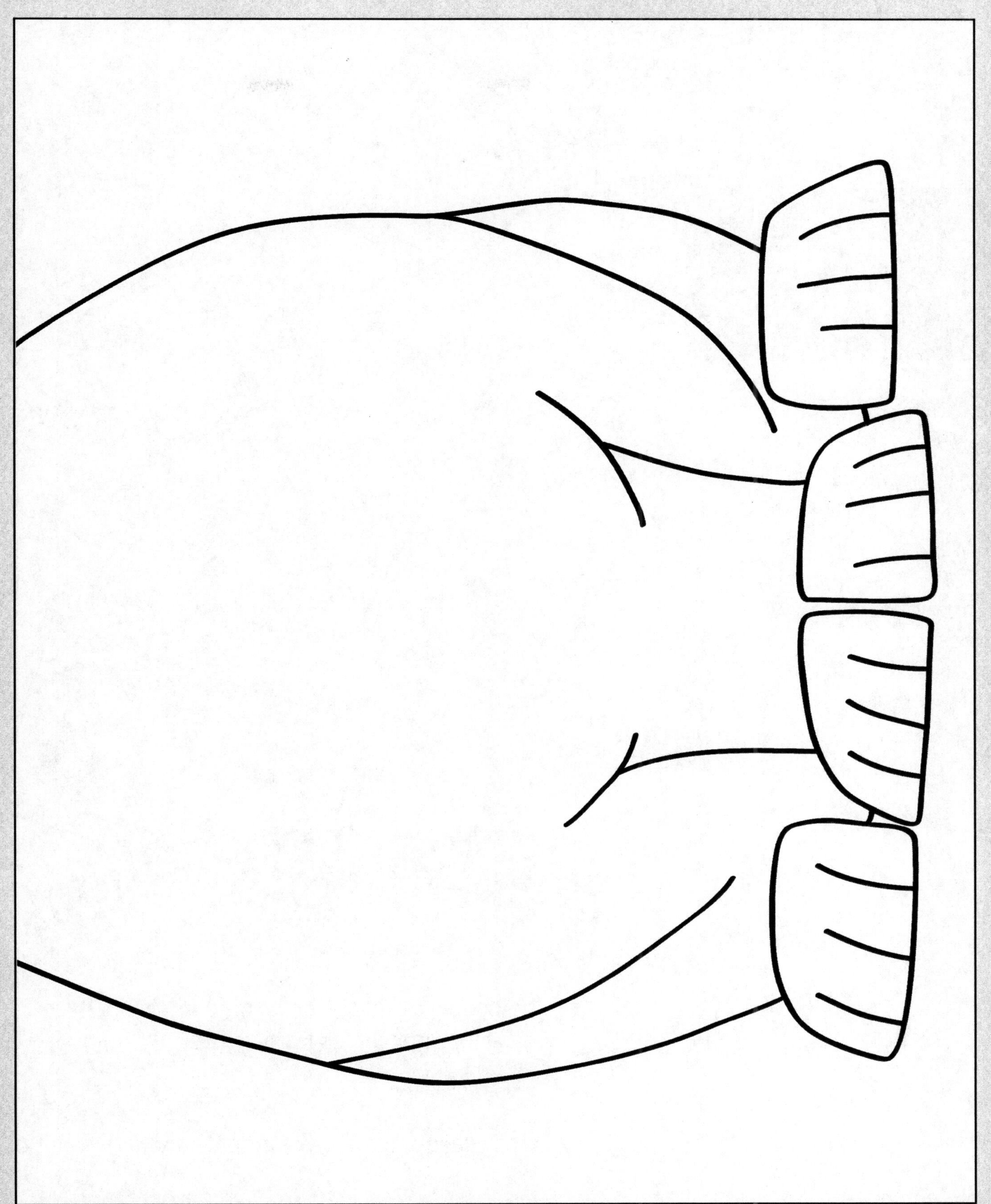

High Dots

Skill:

Counting

Suggested Group Size:

2–6 students

Activity Overview:

Students count dots on dominoes to see who has the most.

Materials:

- "Domino Cards" (pages 104–105)

Activity Preparation

1. Photocopy "Domino Cards" on cardstock paper (or print copies from the CD).
2. Cut out the dominoes.
3. Laminate the dominoes for durability.

Activity Procedure

1. Place all the dominoes facedown in a central location.
2. Have each student select a domino from the stack.
3. Have each student add both sides of the domino together by counting all of the dots. The student with the highest number wins. If two or more students have the same sum, have those students select another domino. Collect the used dominoes.
4. The activity continues until all of the dominoes have been used.

Adaptations

- Have the lowest number win.
- Use real dominoes.
- Have students write or say the addition problem for each domino.
- Have students subtract the lower number from the higher number on their dominoes.

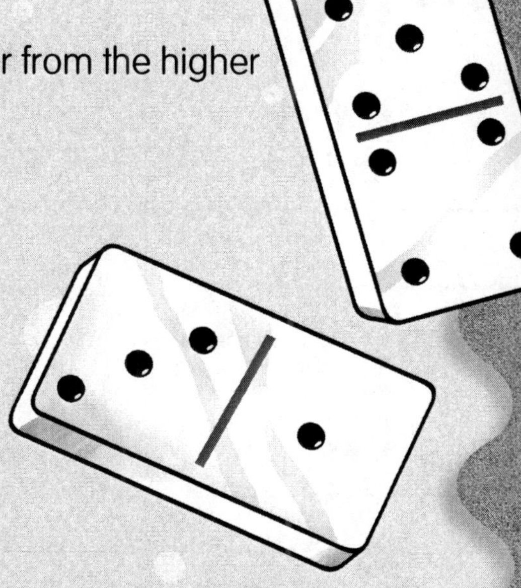

Domino Cards

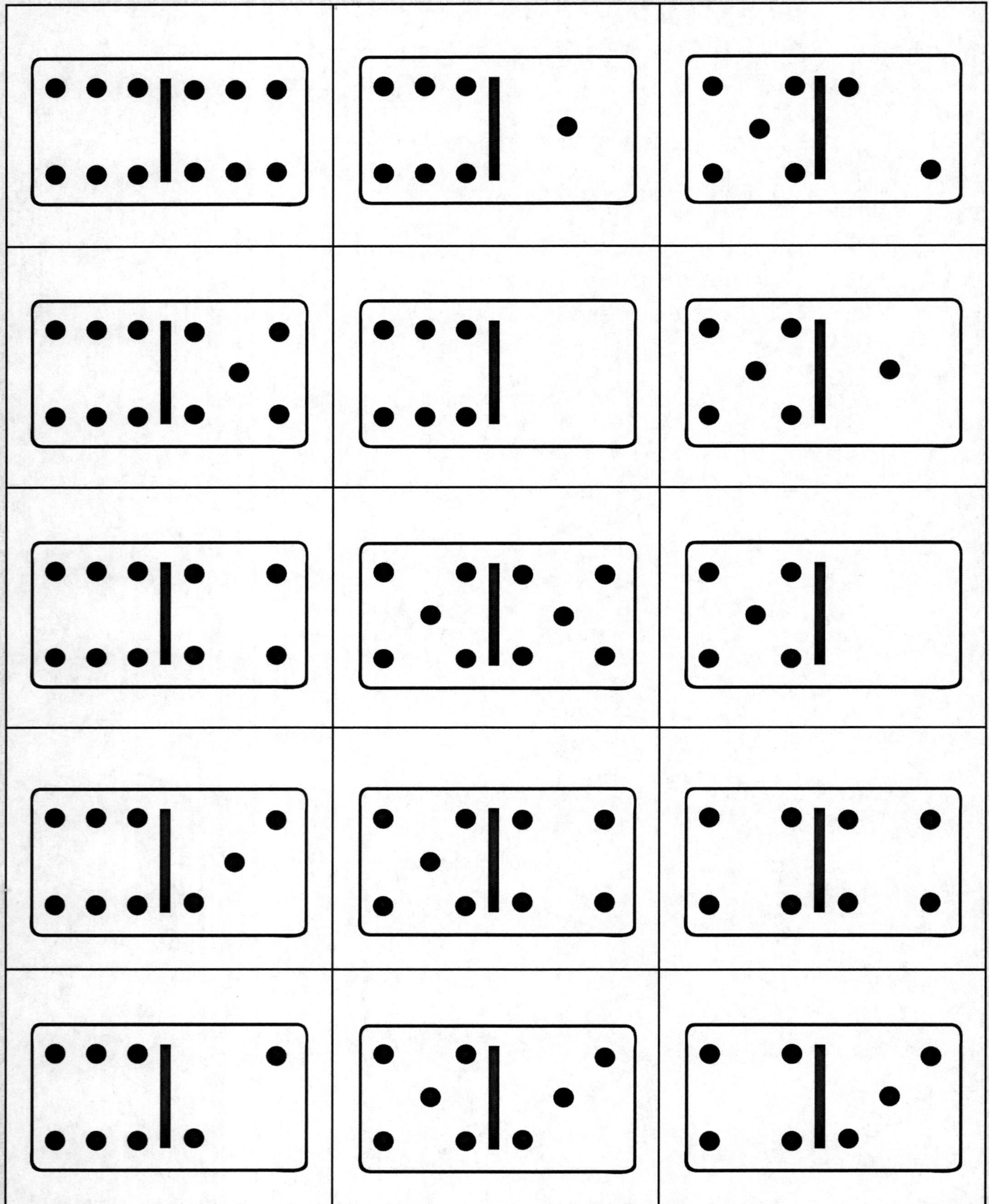

Domino Cards (cont.)

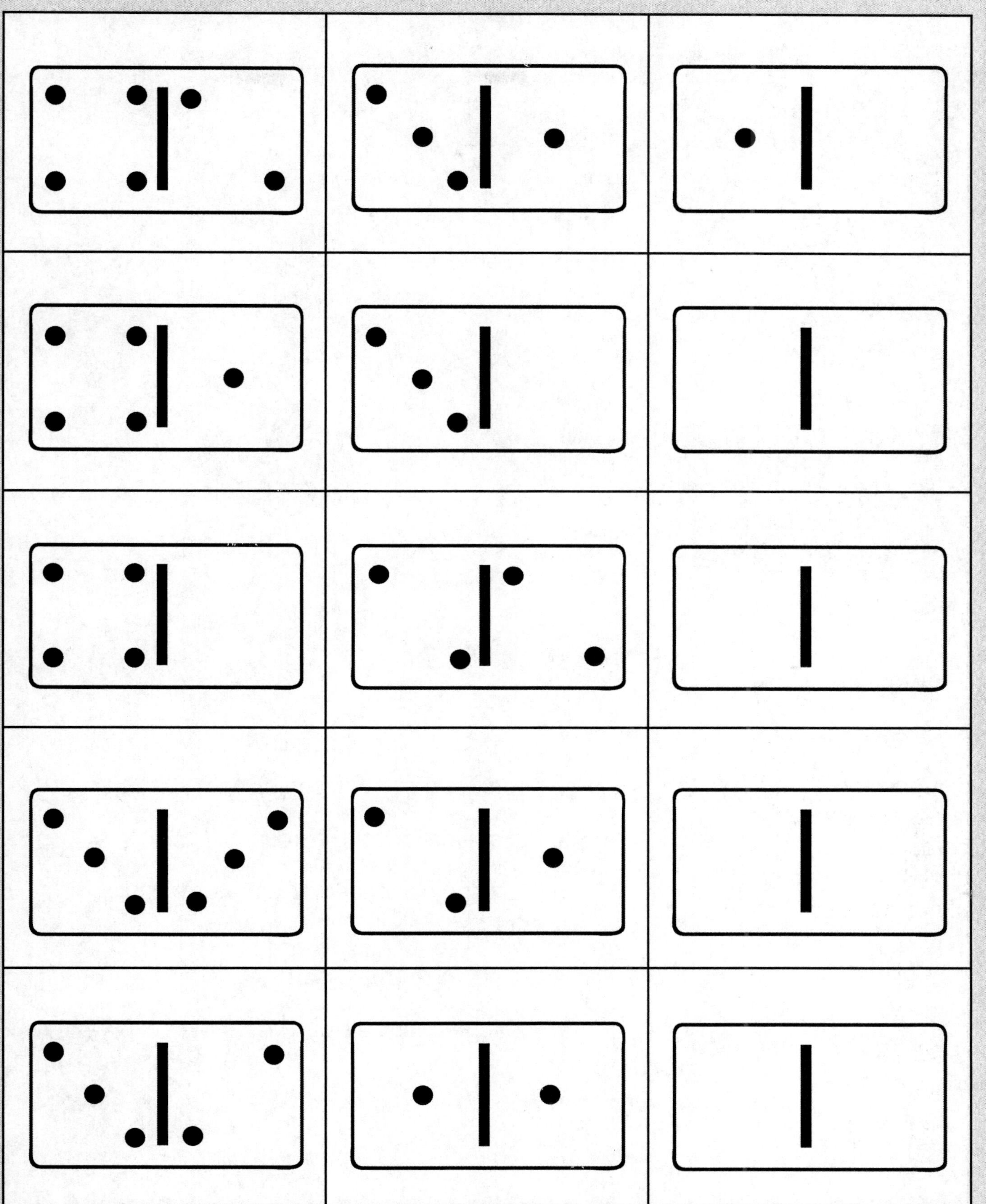

Ladybug Match

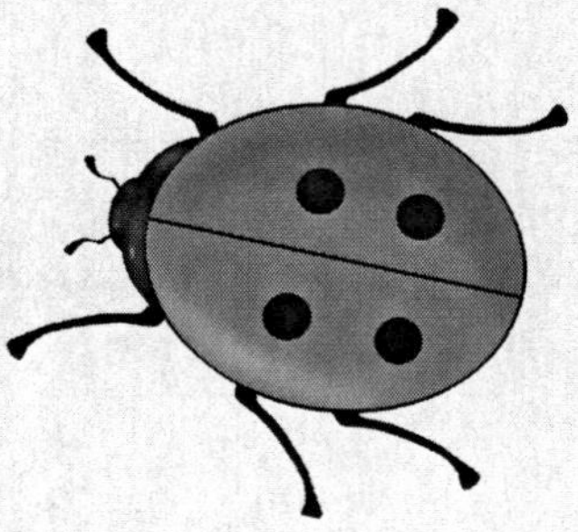

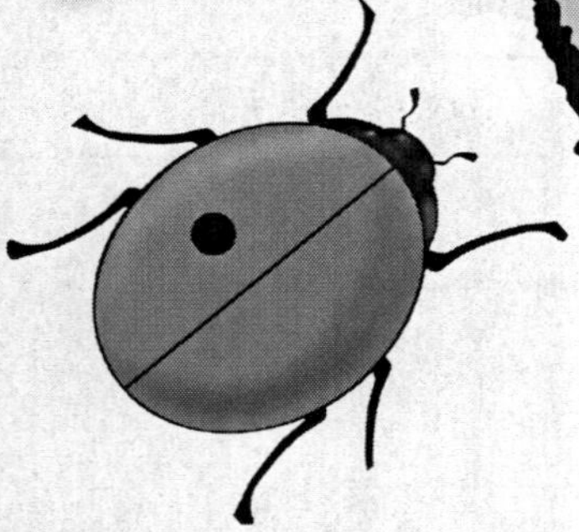

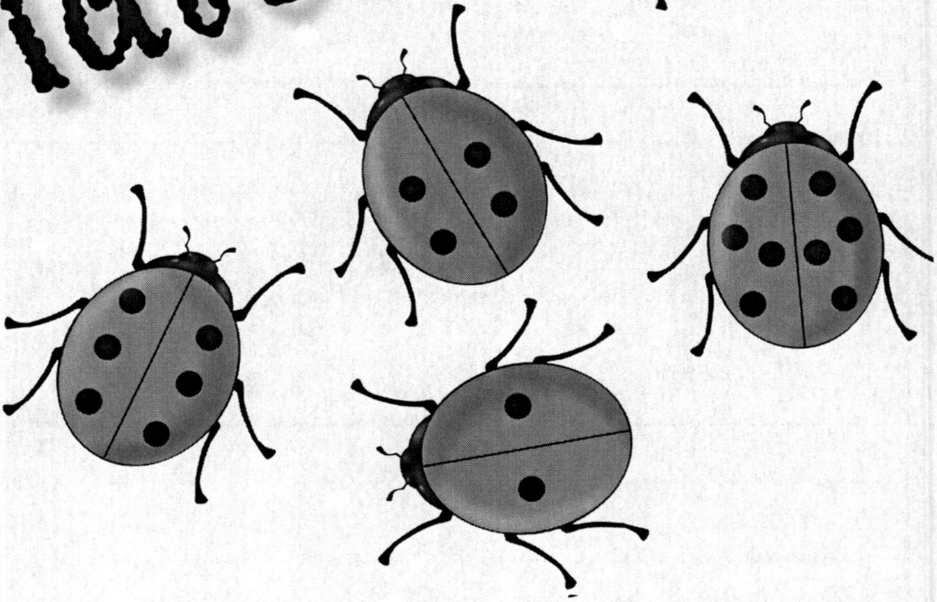

Skill:

Counting

Suggested Group Size:

2–6 students

Activity Overview:

Students match number cards to the ladybug cards that have the corresponding number of dots on them.

Materials:

- "Ladybug Cards" (pages 108–111)
- 1–12 "Number Cards" (pages 169–171)

Activity Preparation

1. Photocopy "Ladybug Cards" on cardstock paper (or print color copies from the CD).
2. Cut out the ladybug cards.
3. Photocopy "Number Cards" on cardstock paper.
4. Cut out the number cards.
5. Laminate both sets of cards for durability.

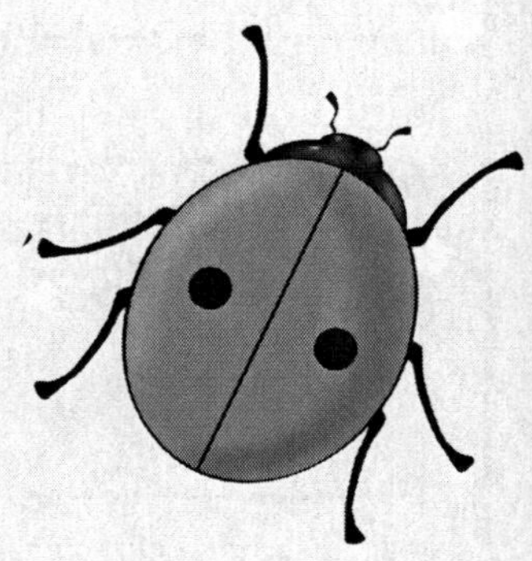

Activity Procedure

1. Shuffle the number cards and place them facedown in rows on the left side of the playing area.
2. Shuffle the ladybug cards and place them facedown in rows on the right side of the playing area.
3. Have a student select and turn over one number card and one ladybug card. If the number on the number card corresponds to the number of dots on the ladybug card, the student has a match. The student keeps the match and another student takes a turn. If a match does not occur, then the student turns both cards back over and another student takes a turn. The activity continues until all of the cards have been matched.

Adaptations

- Omit the ladybug cards. Make two copies of the number cards and follow the same procedure, having students match like numbers.
- Use the domino cards (pages 104–105) instead of the ladybug cards.
- When a student turns a number card over, have him or her count aloud to that number.

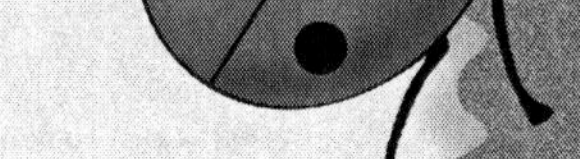

Ladybug Cards

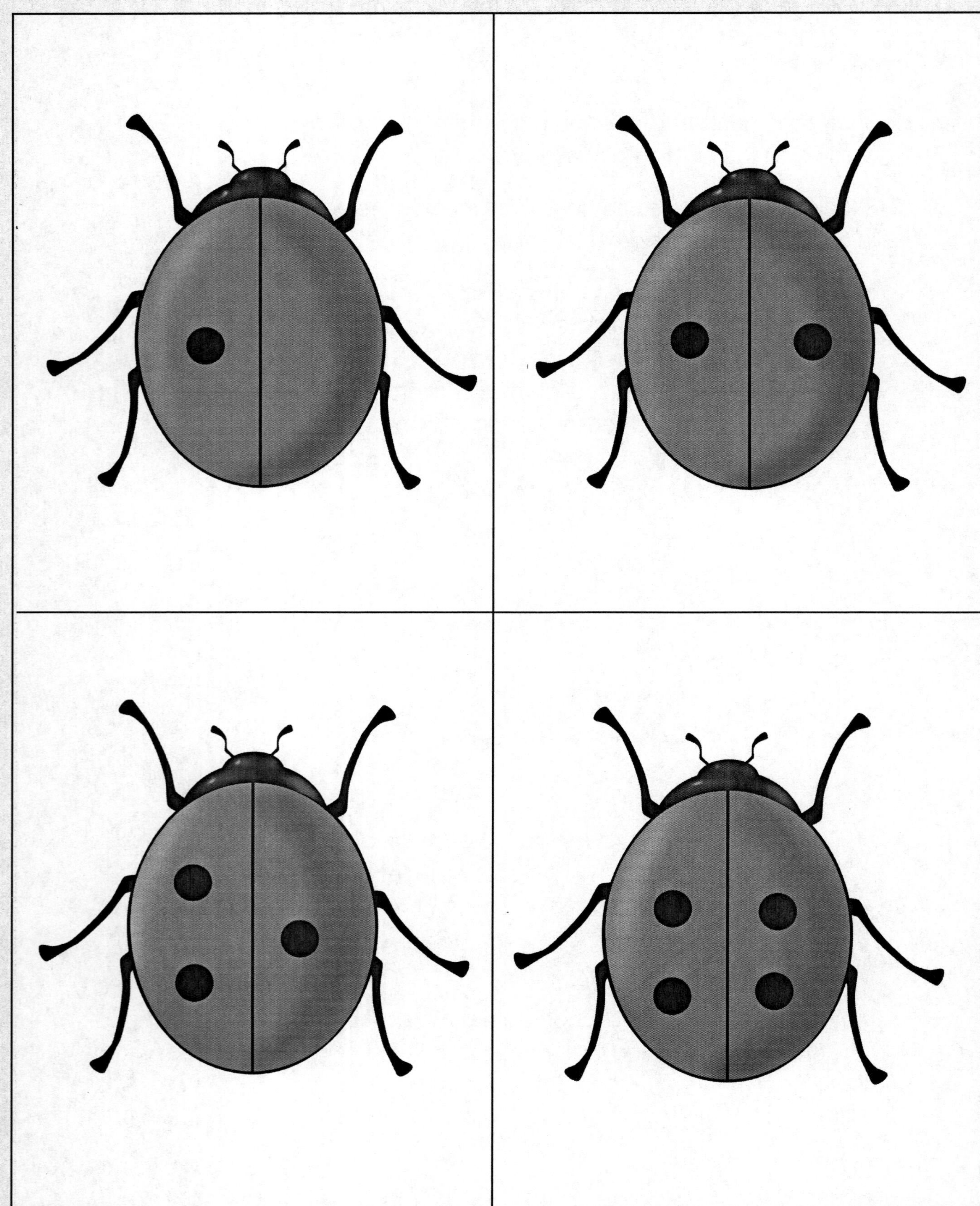

Ladybug Cards (cont.)

Ladybug Cards (cont.)

Ladybug Cards (cont.)

More and Fewer

Skill:

More and fewer

Suggested Group Size:

2–4 students

Activity Overview:

Students compare towers to see which one has more and which one has fewer cubes.

Materials:

- "Number Spinners" (page 114)
- "More or Fewer Mat" (page 115)
- paper clip
- pencil
- connecting cubes

Activity Preparation

1. Photocopy "Number Spinners" on cardstock (or print color copies from the CD).
2. Cut on the dotted line to create two spinner cards.
3. Laminate the spinners for durability.
4. Photocopy "More or Fewer Mat" on cardstock paper (or print color copies from the CD).
5. Decide which number spinner students will use.

Activity Procedure

1. Place the number spinner, paper clip, pencil, and connecting cubes in a central location.

Activity Procedure (cont.)

2. Demonstrate for the students how to use the spinner. Place the paper clip in the center of the circle. Then, put the tip of the pencil on the X. Spin the paper clip around the pencil.
3. Allow students some time to practice using the spinner.
4. Begin the activity by having a student spin the spinner. He or she then builds a tower, using the same number of connecting cubes as the number shown on the spinner. Set the tower aside.
5. Have the student spin the spinner again and build another tower, showing the new number.
6. Have the student compare the two towers to see which one has more cubes and which one has fewer cubes. If the towers have the same number of cubes, have the students spin the spinner again to create one more tower.
7. Have the student place the towers in the correct spaces on the "More or Fewer Mat."
8. Follow the same procedure, providing other students with opportunities to build and compare towers. The activity is over when each student has made five comparisons.

Adaptations

- Use the spinner with larger numbers on it.
- Have two students work together. Each student can build one tower. The students can then compare the two towers and place them on the "More or Fewer Mat."
- Use the "More or Fewer Mat" with number cards rather than towers.
- Use the spinners for addition problems. Have the students spin the spinner twice and add the numbers together.

Number Spinners

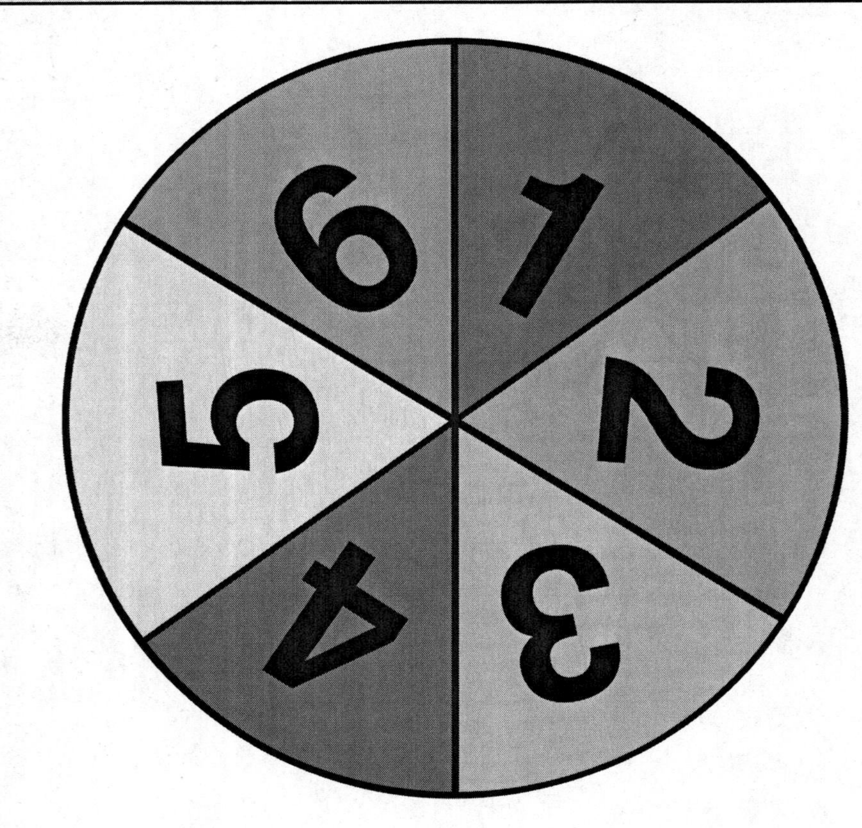

More or Fewer Mat

more	fewer

Make 10

Skill:

Making sets of ten

Suggested Group Size:

2–4 students

Activity Overview:

Students create groups of 10 on a tens tray.

Materials:

- "Tens Tray Pattern" (page 118)
- nine blue connecting cubes
- 10 red connecting cubes
- plastic zipper bag
- box lid or tray

1. Photocopy "Tens Tray Pattern" on cardstock paper (or print copies from the CD).
2. Laminate for durability.
3. Place the nine blue connecting cubes into the plastic zipper bag.
4. Place the 10 red connecting cubes in the box lid or tray.

Activity Procedure

1. Place the zipper bag and tray of connecting cubes in a central location.
2. Display the tens tray and have students count the boxes. Count the boxes on the tens tray several times, if needed, until students understand that there are 10 boxes.
3. Have a student reach into the zipper bag and take out a handful of connecting cubes and count them out loud.
4. Ask the student to place the connecting cubes on the tens tray so that one connecting cube is in each box.
5. Have the student determine how many more cubes would be needed to make 10. If necessary, allow the student to fill the empty boxes with red cubes from the box lid or tray.
6. Ask the student which has more: the tray with blue cubes or the tray with red cubes.
7. Continue following the same procedure as other students in the group take a turn. The activity is over when each student has had five turns, or as time allows.

Adaptations

- Provide only the blue cubes for students. Have them mentally determine how many spaces are left to fill on the tens tray.
- Have students fill the tens tray with the same-colored cubes. Then, have the student close his or her eyes while you take some away. Have the student determine how many cubes were taken away based on how many are left.
- Use "Fives Tray Patterns" (page 119) to practice with smaller numbers.

Tens Tray Pattern

Fives Tray Patterns

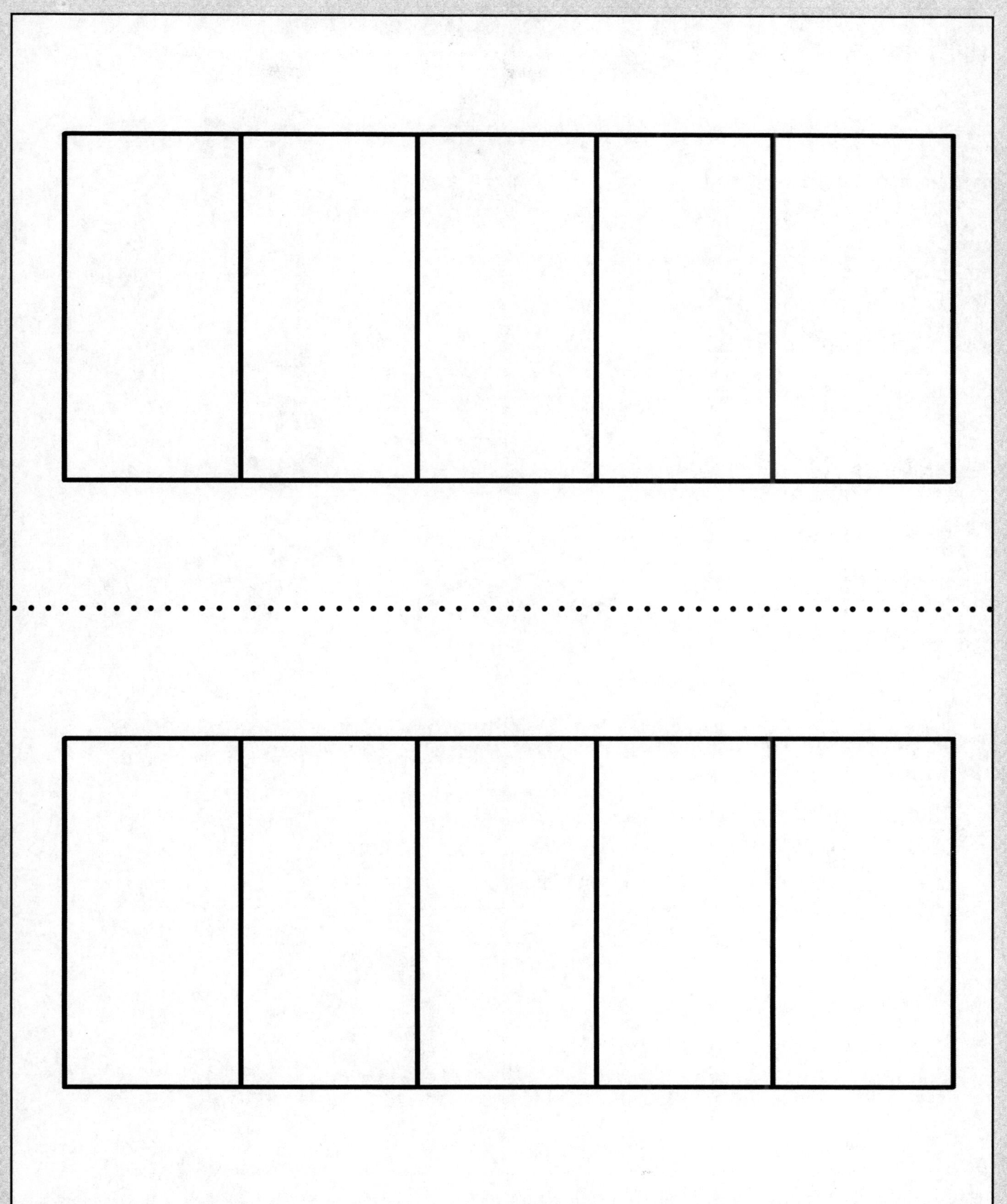

Missing Number

Skill:

Sequencng numbers

Suggested Group Size:

2–4 students

Activity Overview:

Students supply the missing number in a sequence of numbers.

Materials:

- "Sequence Cards" (pages 122–126)
- "Numbered Playing Cards" (page 127)

Activity Preparation

1. Photocopy "Sequence Cards" and "Numbered Playing Cards" on cardstock paper (or print copies from the CD).
2. Cut out the cards.
3. Laminate the cards for durability.

Activity Procedure

1. Shuffle the numbered playing cards and deal five cards to each student. Place the remaining number cards facedown on the table.

2. Shuffle the sequence cards and set them aside so the students do not get them confused with the number cards.

3. Determine which student will go first.

4. Display one sequence card. The student must look at the number cards in his or her hand and determine whether he or she has a card with the missing number. If the student does have the missing number, he or she can collect the sequence card and lay it on the table with the corresponding number play card. If the student does not have the missing number, he or she must draw another number card.

5. Continue playing following the same procedure. The activity is over when a student has no more number cards in his or her hands.

Adaptations

- Have students lay their numbered playing cards on the desk rather than hold them in their hands.
- Write the missing number on the backs of the sequence cards. Students can do the activity independently and self-check the answers.
- Continue playing until all the sequence cards have been matched with all the number cards.
- Have students practice only numbers 1–5. Sort through both the sequence cards and numbered playing cards to eliminate any cards with numbers greater than five.

Sequence Cards

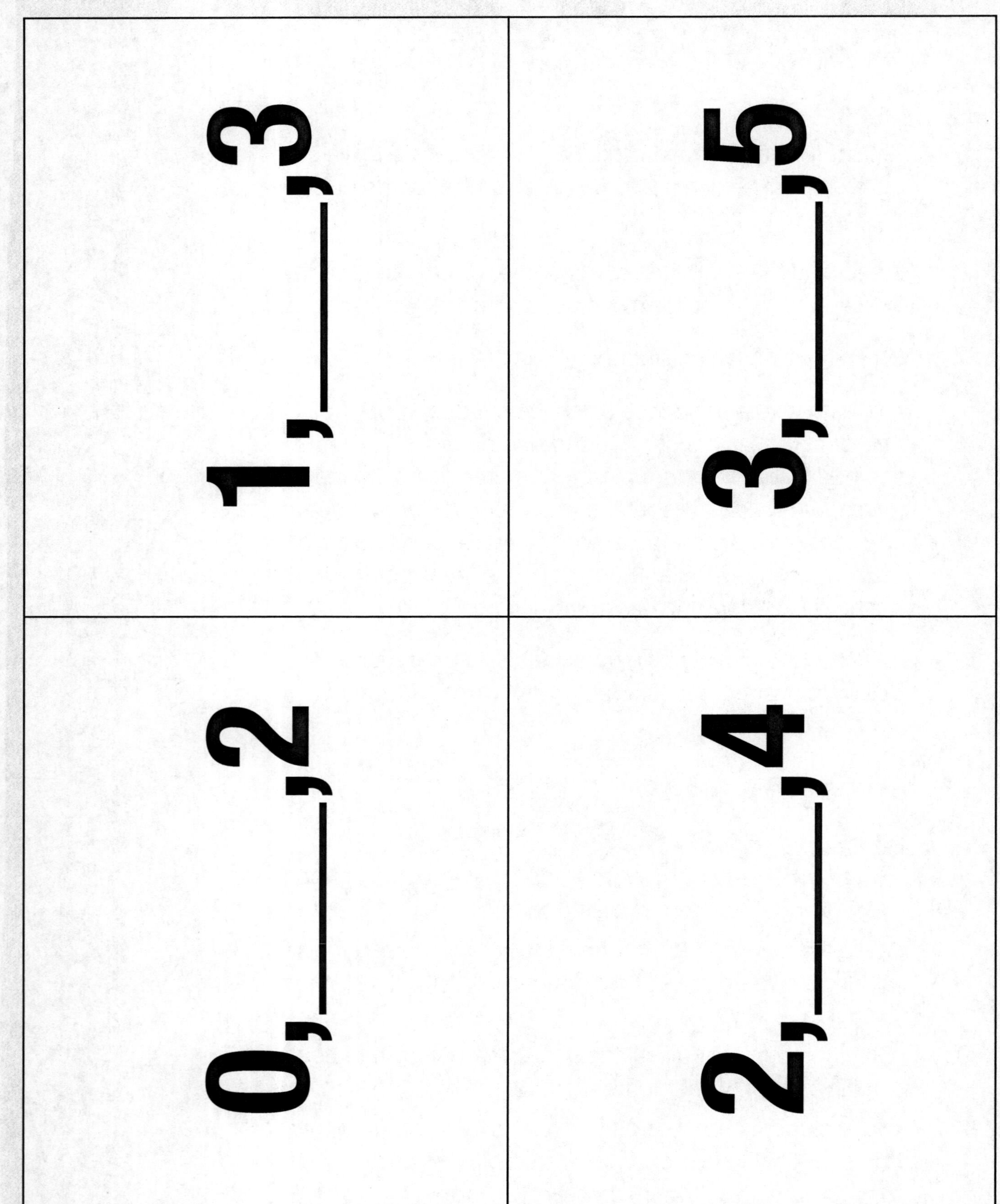

Sequence Cards (cont.)

5, ___, 7	7, ___, 9
4, ___, 6	6, ___, 8

___, 2, 3	___, 4, 5
8, ___, 10	___, 3, 4

3, 4, ___	5, 6, ___
___, 5, 6	___, 7, 8

Sequence Cards (cont.)

7, 8, ___	9, ___, 11
___, 9, 10	8, 9, ___

Numbered Playing Cards

10	10
9	9
8	8
7	7
6	6
5	5
4	4
3	3
2	2
1	1

Jump the Line

Skill:

Adding

Suggested Group Size:

2–4 students

Activity Overview:

Students demonstrate addition by jumping on a number line.

Materials:

- 0–5 "Number Cards" (pages 168–170)
- 10 ft (3 m) of butcher paper
- black marker
- yardstick or meter stick
- small white- or chalkboard
- whiteboard marker or chalk
- an eraser

Activity Preparation

1. Photocopy two sets of the 0–5 "Number Cards" on cardstock paper.
2. Cut out the cards.
3. Laminate the cards for durability.
4. Create an oversized number line by drawing a horizontal line 10 feet (3 meters) long down the middle of the butcher paper. Draw short vertical lines at every foot (30 cm).
5. Write the numbers 1–10 next to the short vertical lines, one number per line.
6. Laminate the number line for durability.

Activity Procedure

1. Lay the oversized number line on the floor in a clear area.
2. Shuffle the number cards and place them facedown in a central location.
3. Have a student stand at the beginning of the number line.
4. Take the top card from the deck of cards and display it for the student to see.
5. Have the student jump down the number line to the number shown on the card.
6. Take a second card from the deck of cards and display it for the student to see.
7. Tell him or her to jump that many more spaces on the number line.
8. Have the student remain on the number he or she jumped to as you write down the number sentences on a white- or chalkboard to show what happened. (For example, 2 + 4 = 6.)

Adaptations

- Have two students act out the problem together. Have one student jump to the first number. Have the second student begin where the first student left off and jump to show the second number.
- Draw two cards. Have the student begin on the larger number and jump backward down the number line to represent subtracting the smaller number. Write the number sentence.

Add One

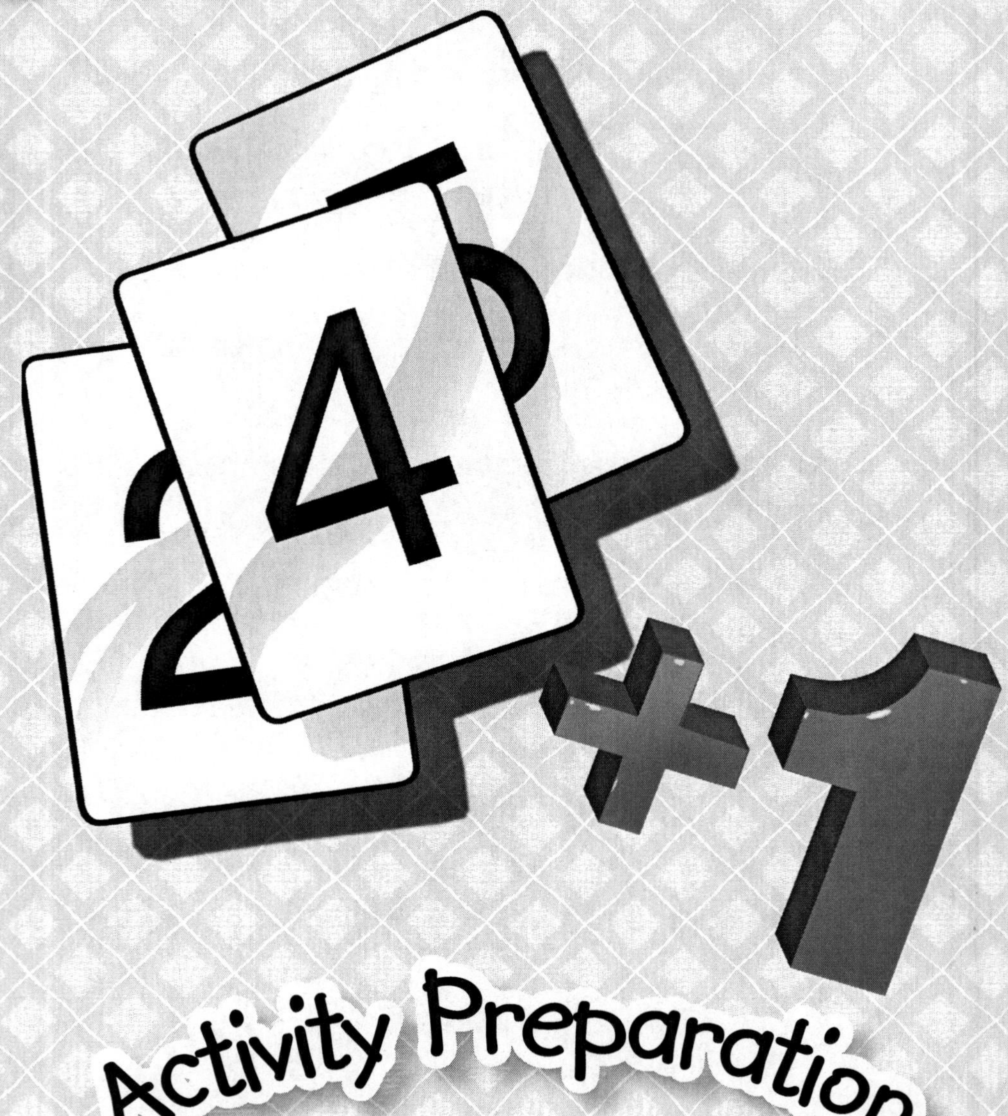

Skill:

Adding

Suggested Group Size:

2–4 students

Activity Overview:

Students add one number onto cards they select and color the matching number on a game mat.

Materials:

- "21 Game Mat" (page 132)
- 0–20 "Number Cards" (pages 168–173)
- a crayon or marker

Activity Preparation

1. Photocopy "21 Game Mat" (or print copies from the CD).
2. Photocopy 0–20 "Number Cards" on cardstock paper.
3. Cut out the number cards.
4. Laminate the number cards for durability.

Activity Procedure

1. Place the "21 Game Mat" and a marker or crayon in a central location.
2. Shuffle the number cards and place them facedown in a central location.
3. Have a student take the top card from the card deck.
4. Have the student add one to the number shown on the card. The student then colors the box on the game mat that contains that number.
5. Have other students take turns following the same procedure. The activity is over when all the boxes on the game mat have been colored.

Adaptations

- Provide each student with his or her own game mat.
- Use two dice and the "13 Game Mat" (page 133). Have the student roll the dice and add one to the sum of the two dice.
- Change the activity into a subtraction game. For each card selected, the student will subtract one and color the corresponding box on the game mat. (Color the boxes for numbers 21 and 20 before beginning this activity.)
- Change the activity into a number-identification game. Rather than adding one to the number card drawn, have the student find the matching number on the game mat. (Have students color the box numbered 21 before beginning this activity.)

21 Game Mat

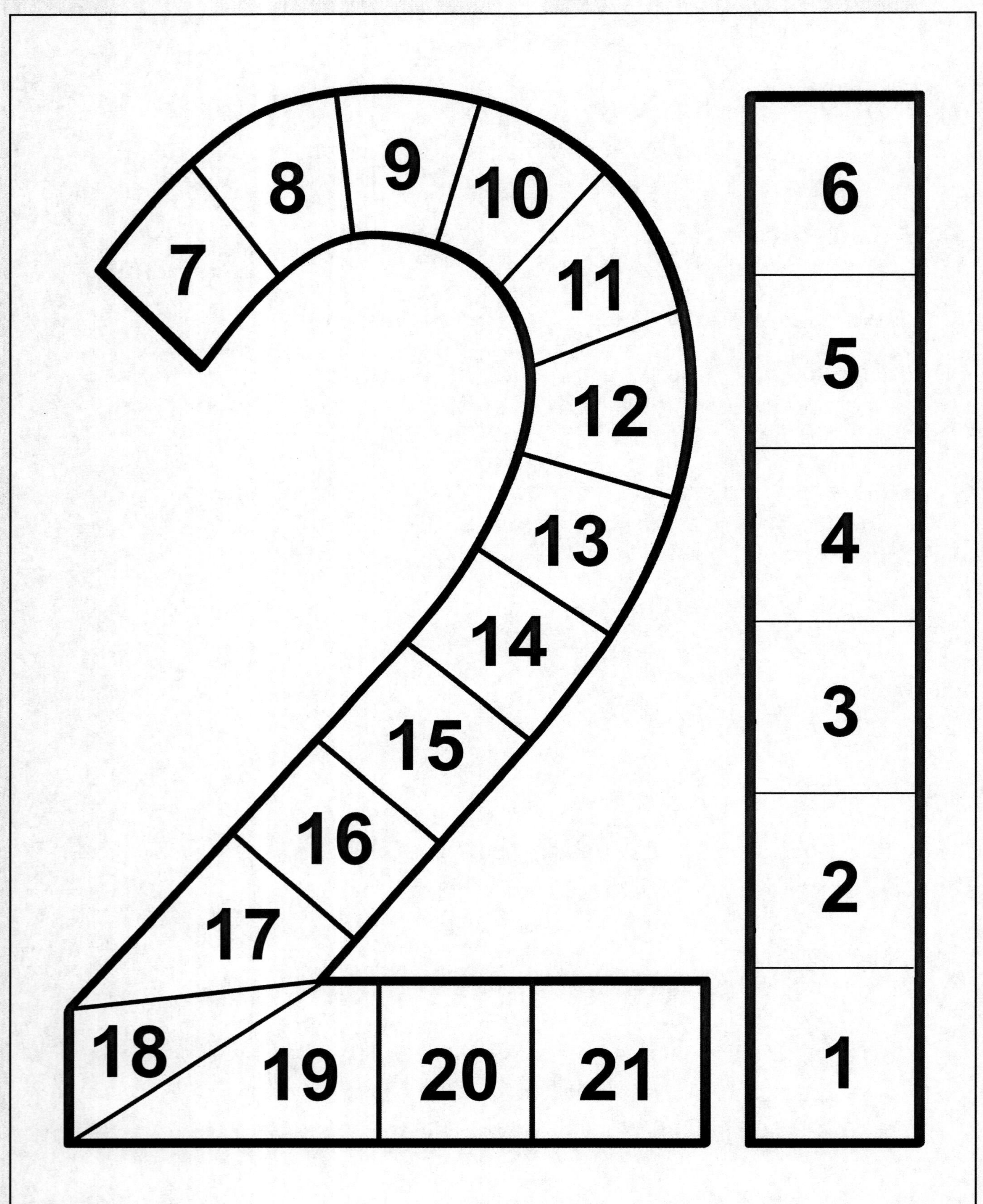

13 Game Mat

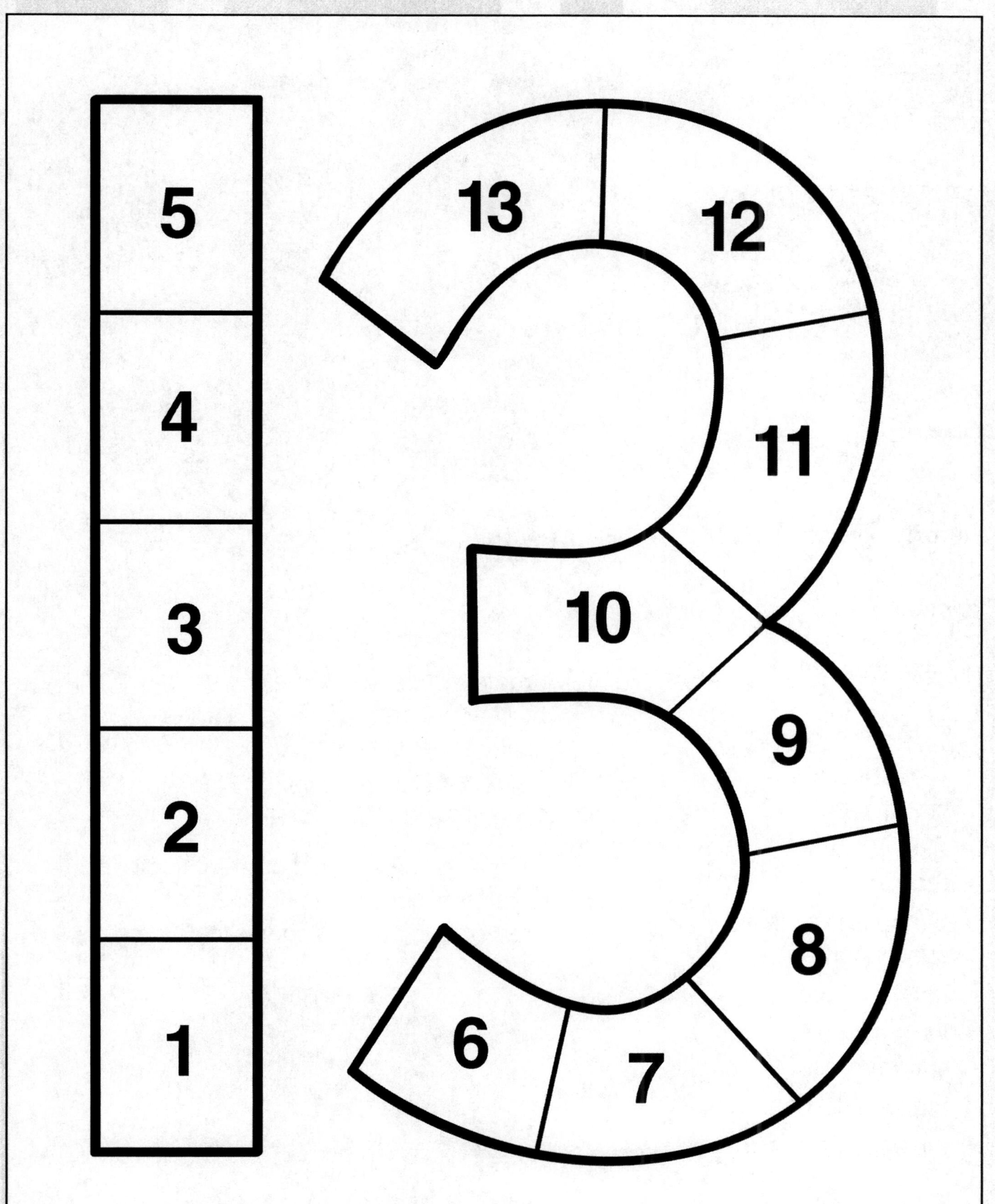

Bull's-Eye!

Skill:

Adding

Suggested Group Size:

2–4 students

Activity Overview:

Students toss beanbags on a game mat and add the numbers together.

Materials:

- 2 x 2 ft (60 cm x 60 cm) sheet of butcher paper
- marker
- beanbags or other space markers
- masking tape
- whiteboards or chalkboards
- markers or chalk
- erasers

Activity Preparation

1. Create a bull's-eye game mat on the butcher paper by drawing a large circle on the sheet of butcher paper. Draw a medium circle within the large circle. Draw a small circle within the medium circle.
2. Label each circle with a different number according to the level of difficulty of problems you want students to practice.

Activity Procedure

1. Put the bull's-eye game mat on the ground.
2. Place masking tape a few feet away to make a standing line.
3. Pair students and provide each pair with a whiteboard or chalkboard and a marker or chalk.
4. Have a student stand on the start line and toss two beanbags on the bull's-eye game mat.
5. Have the student look at the numbers on which each of the beanbags landed. The student then adds the two numbers together and says the sum.
6. The student's partner then records the number sentences on the whiteboard or chalkboard.
7. Allow other pairs of children to play, following the same procedure.

Adaptations

- Change the numbers that are written on the bull's-eye to make the problems more difficult.
- Provide the students with three beanbags. Have the students add all three numbers together.
- Tell the students a starting number, such as 8. Have the students toss only one beanbag and subtract the number on the bulls-eye from the number 8.
- Have students work alone rather than in pairs.

Skill:

Adding

Suggested Group Size:

2–4 students

Activity Overview:

Students match ducks that have addition problems written on them to numbers on their game mats.

Materials:

- "Pond Game Mats 1–4" (pages 138–141)
- "Duck Patterns" (pages 142–145)

1. Photocopy "Pond Game Mats 1–4" on cardstock paper (or print color copies from the CD).
2. Photocopy "Duck Patterns" on cardstock (or print color copies from the CD).
3. Cut out the duck patterns.
4. Laminate the game mats and duck patterns for durability.

Activity Procedure

1. Give each student a game mat.
2. Place the ducks, problem side down, in a central location.
3. Have a student select a duck. Have the student solve the addition problem on the duck. The student must look at the numbers on the lily pads on his or her game mat to see if the answer to the problem is on the game mat. If it is, students may place the duck on the corresponding number. If it is not, then he or she must place the duck back with the other ducks.
4. Have other students take turns following the same procedure. The game is over when all the lily pads have ducks on them.

Adaptations

- Use little rubber ducks as the space markers on the ponds.
- Have each student read the problem and say the answer to the addition problem out loud before placing it on his or her game mat.
- Use the number cards (pages 168–173) to create a number-matching game.
- Use the same number cards as the numbers on the lily pads.
- Create dot cards that correspond to the numbers written on the lily pads. Have students count the dots on the cards and match the cards to the numbers on the lily pads.

1+1 1+2 1+3

Duck Pond Game Mat – 1

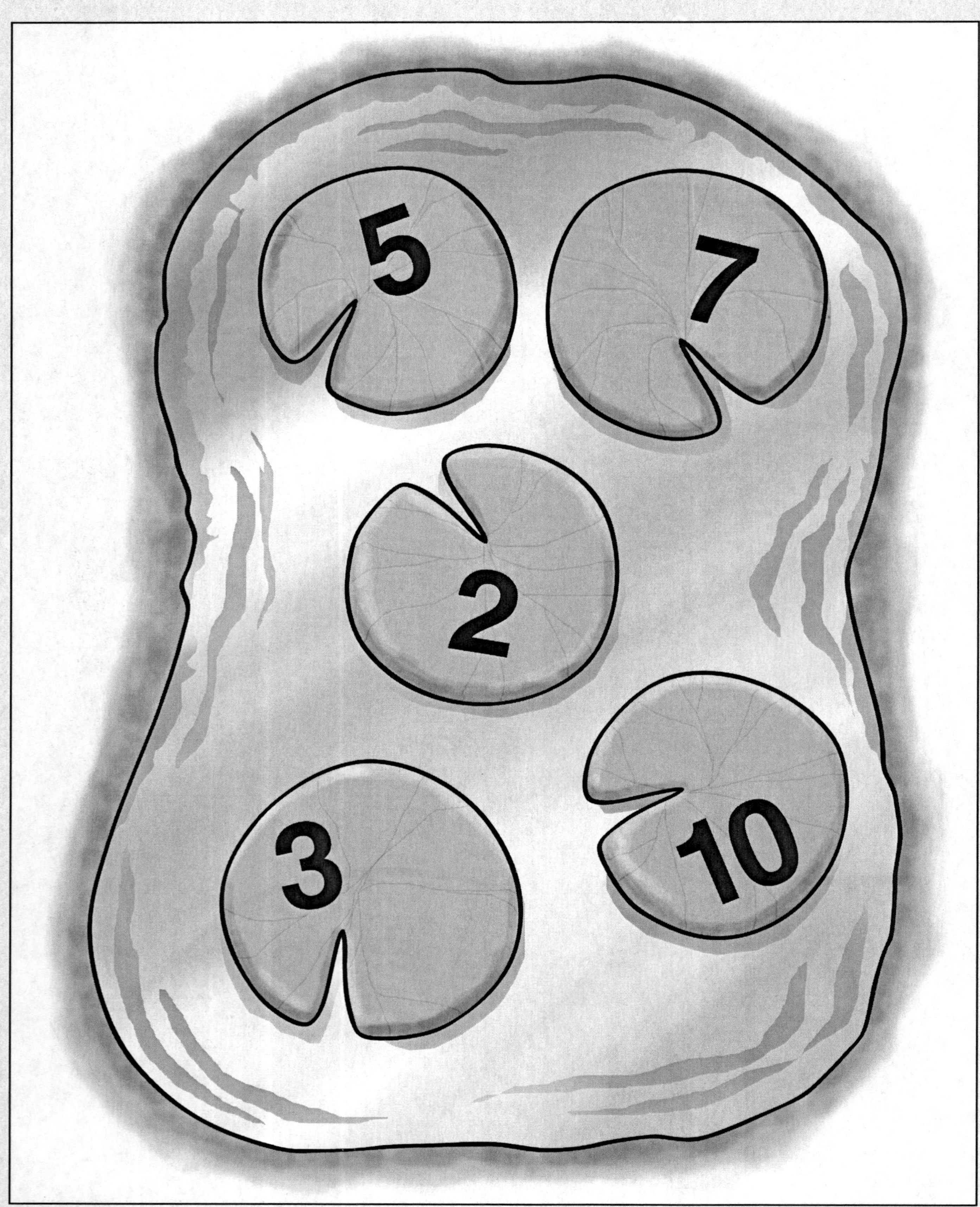

Duck Pond Game Mat – 2

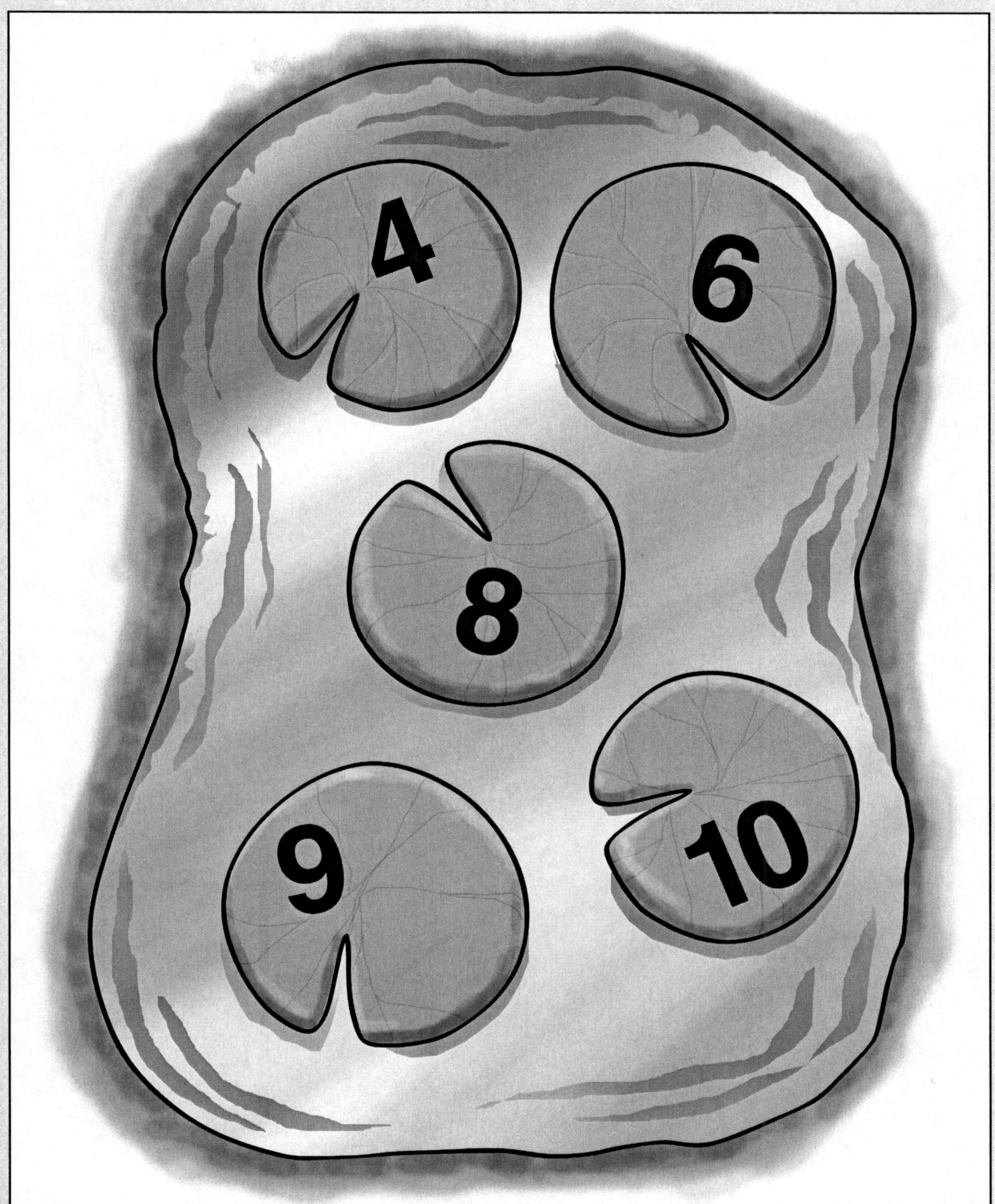

Duck Pond Game Mat – 3

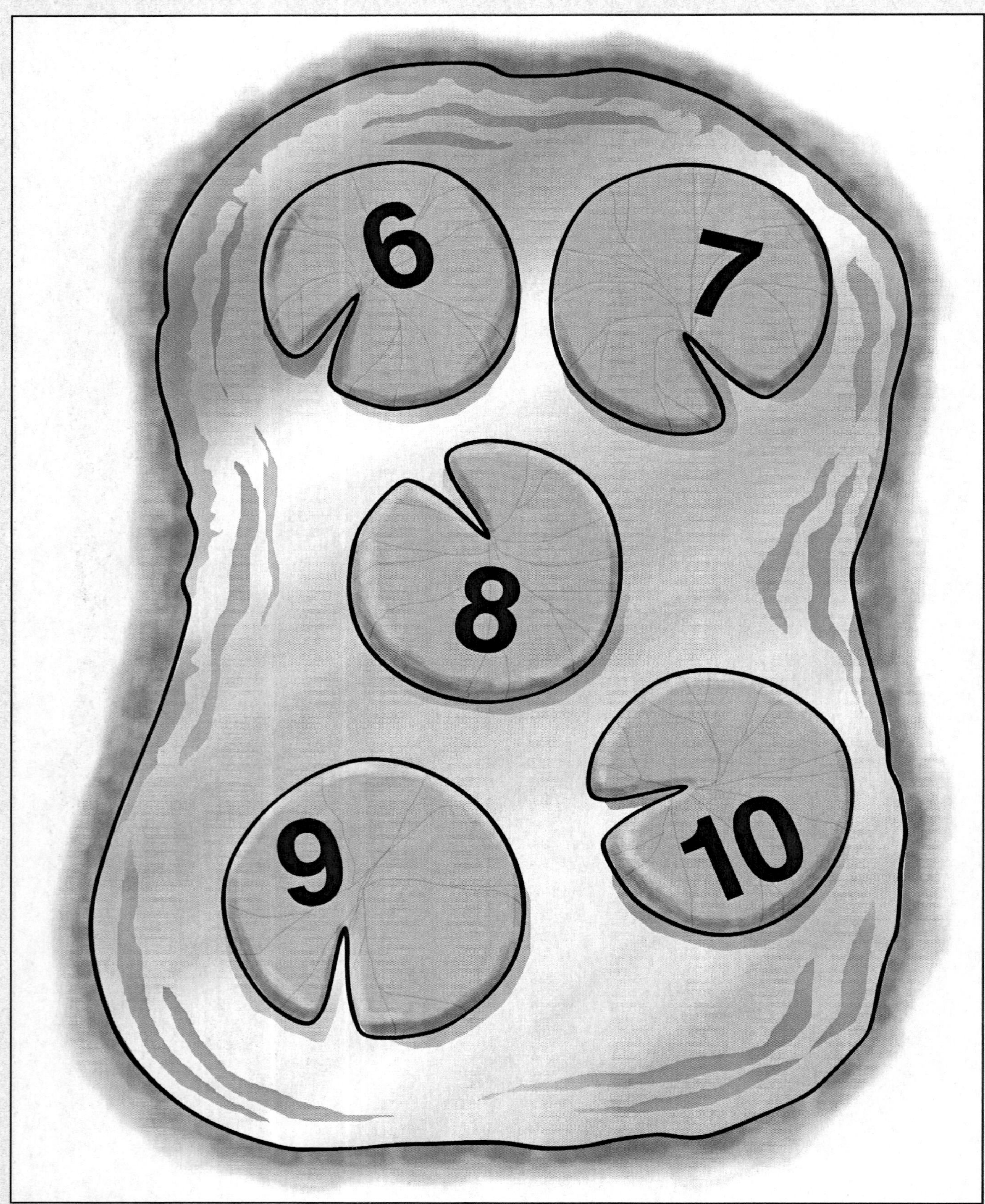

Duck Pond Game Mat – 4

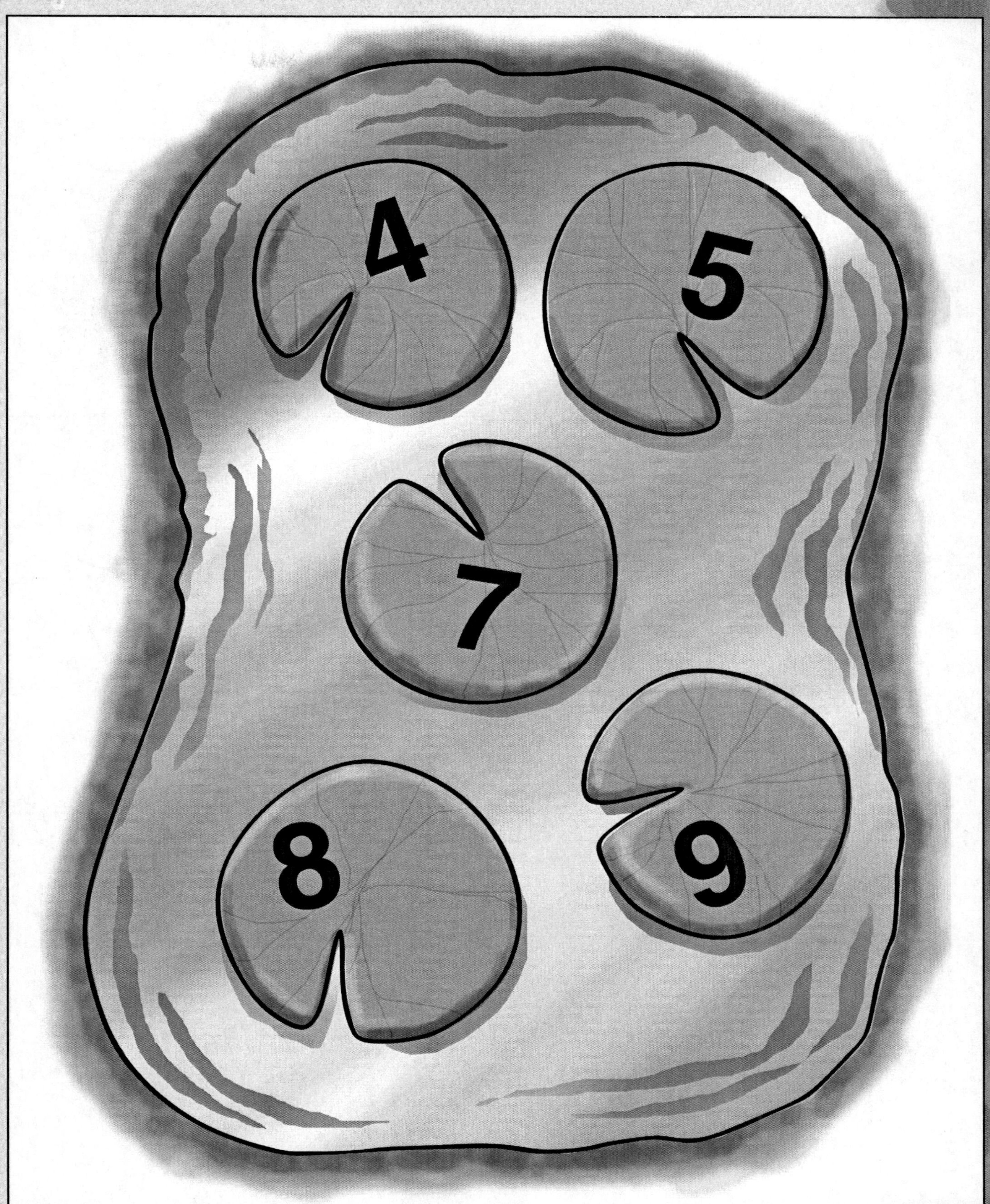

Duck Patterns

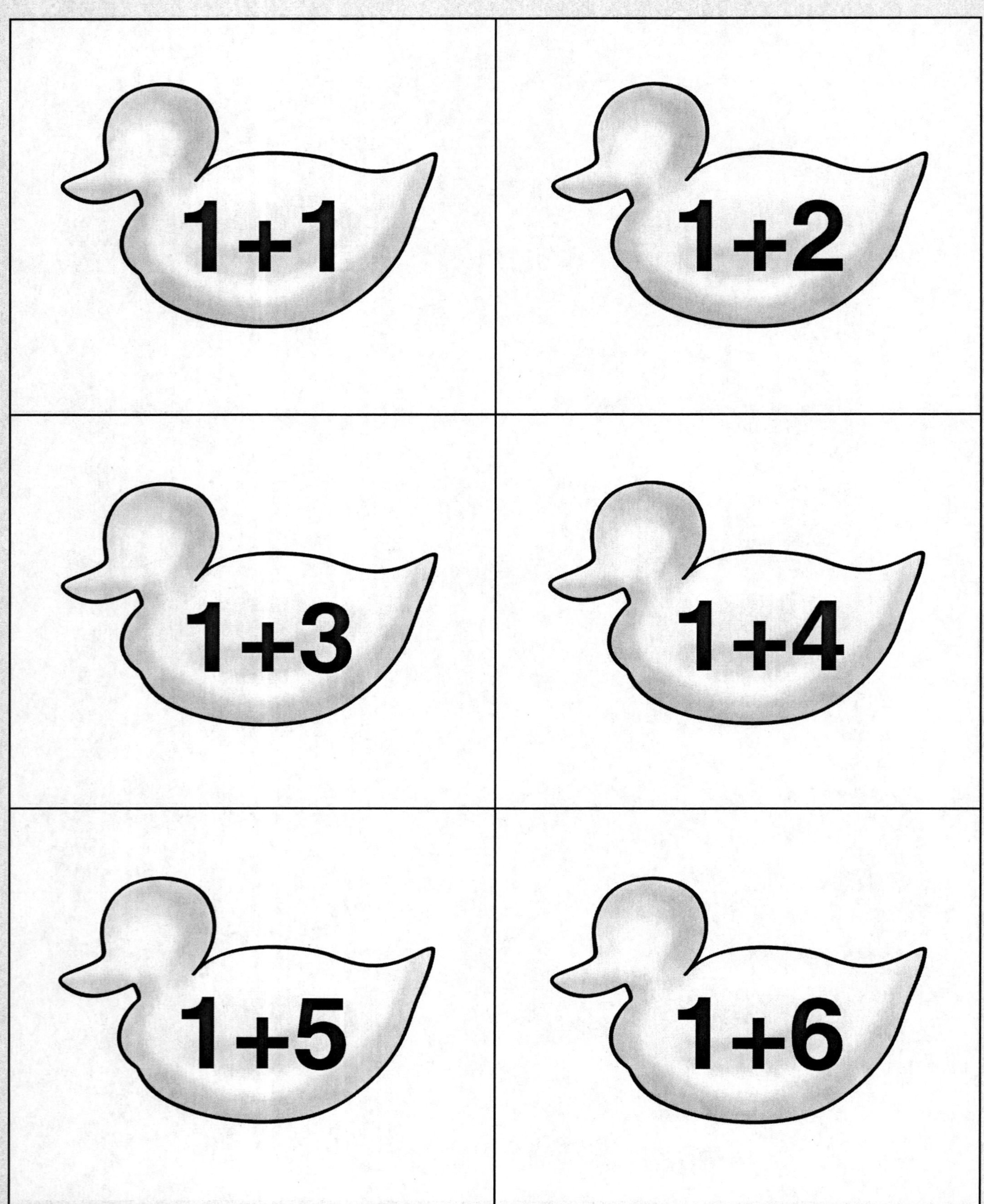

Duck Patterns (cont.)

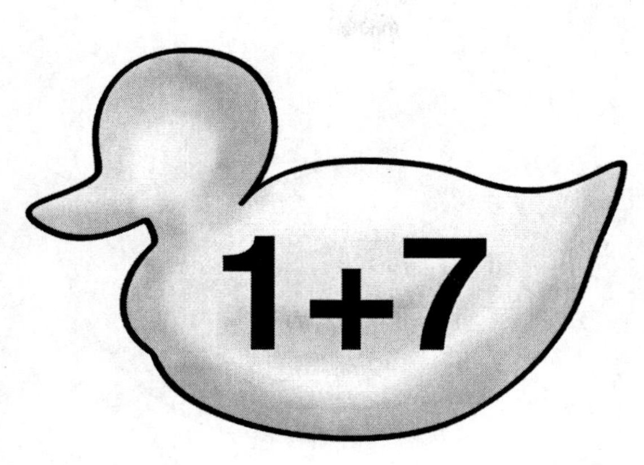

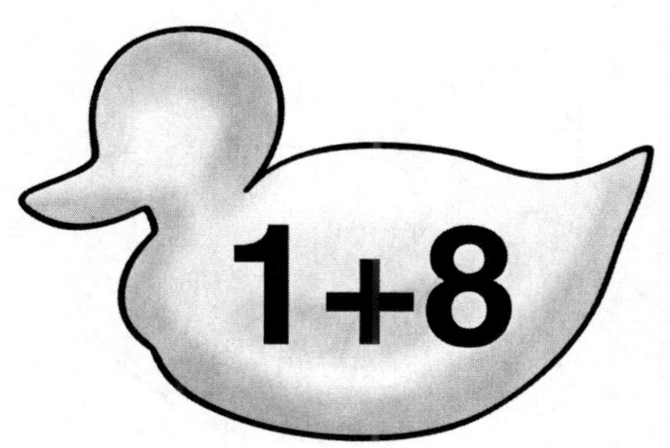

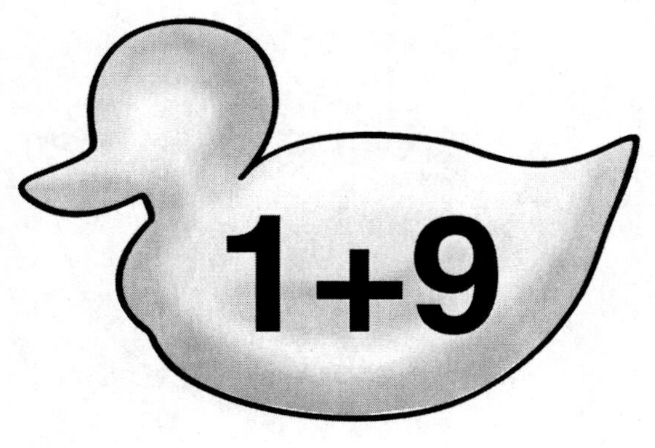

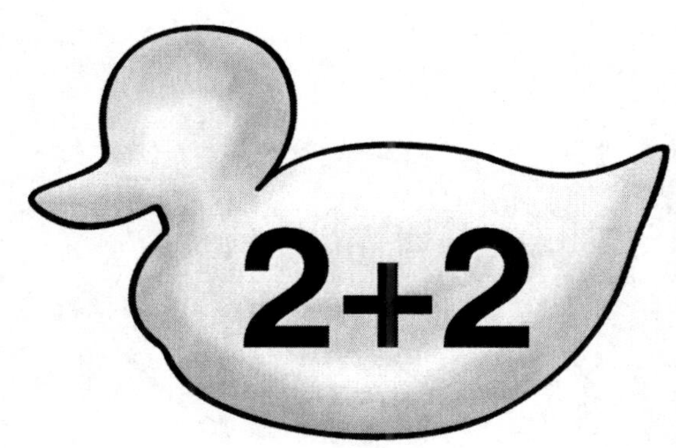

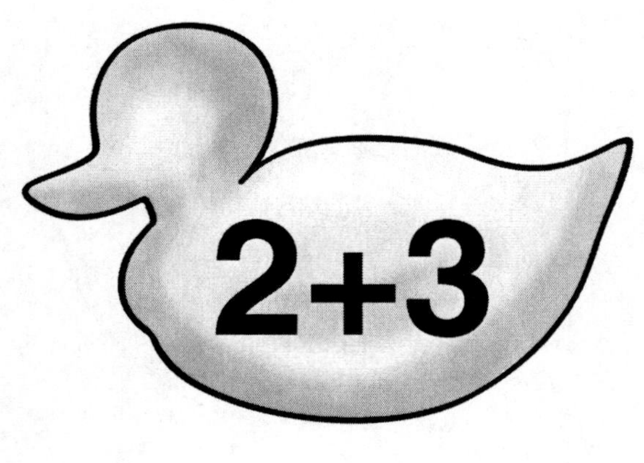

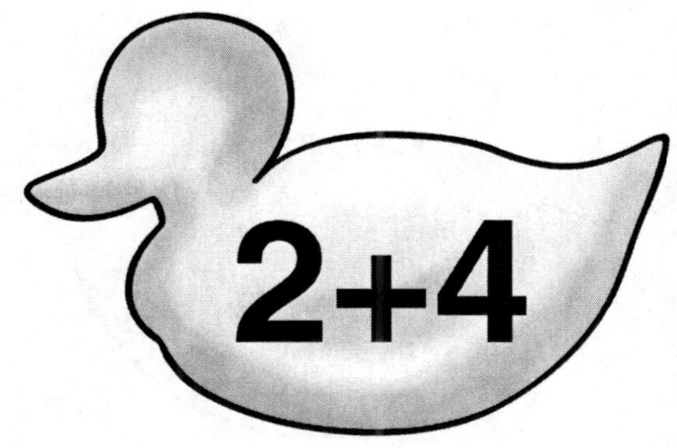

Duck Patterns (cont.)

Duck Patterns (cont.)

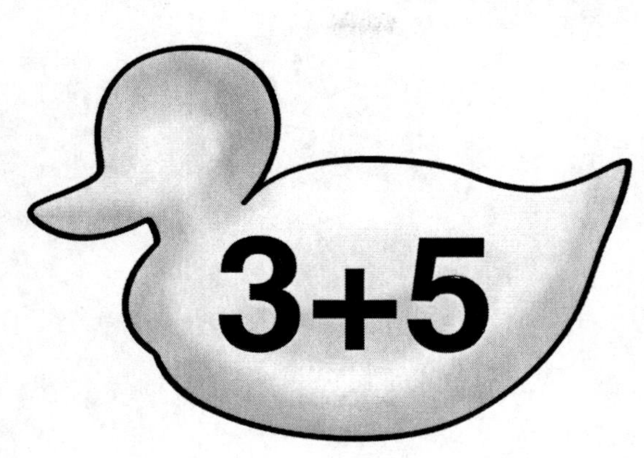

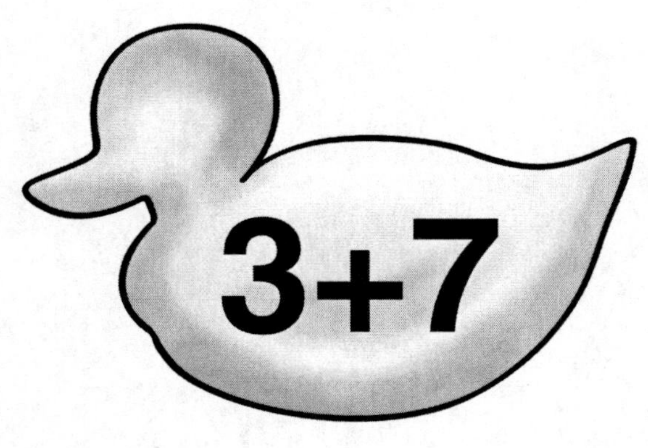

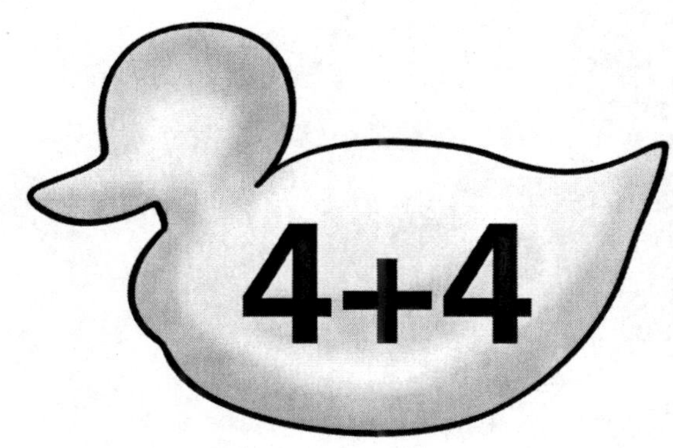

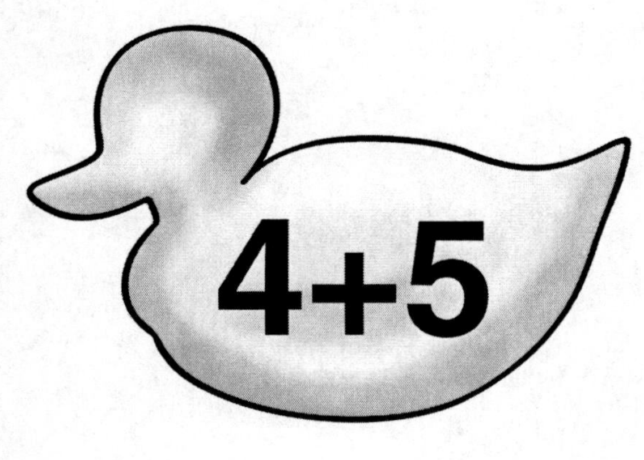

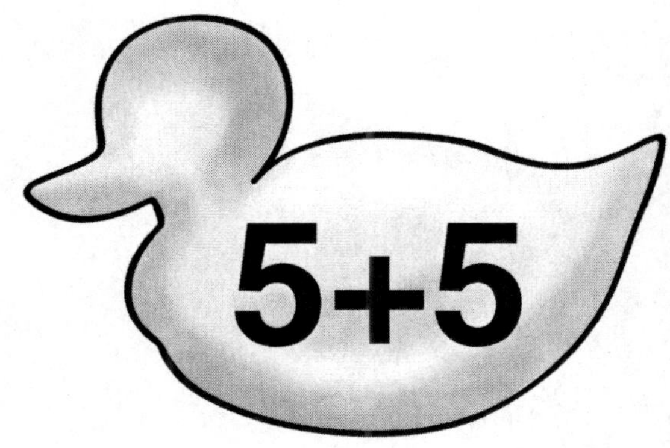

Pepperoni Plus

Activity Preparation

1. Photocopy "Pizza Pattern," one per student (or print copies from the CD).

2. Photocopy multiple sets of 0–3 "Number Cards."

Skill:

Adding

Suggested Group Size:

2–4 students

Activity Overview:

Students color pieces of pepperoni on their own pizzas, based on addition problems.

Materials:

- "Pizza Pattern" (page 148)
- 0–3 "Number Cards" (page 168–169)
- crayons or markers

Activity Procedure

1. Give each student a pizza pattern and a crayon or marker.
2. Place the shuffled 0–3 cards facedown in a central location.
3. Have a student select the top two cards from the 0–3 deck and add the numbers together. The student then colors that same number of pepperoni pieces on his or her own pizza.
4. Have other students take turns following the same procedure. When only a few pieces of pepperoni remain uncolored, a student must select two cards with a sum equal to the number of pieces left on his or her pizza. The activity is over once all the students have colored all their pepperoni.

Adaptations

- Use a die and have students color pieces of pepperoni corresponding to the number that is rolled.
- Use a die or the 0–6 cards instead of the 0–3 cards.
- Use the 0–6 cards and have students find the difference between the two cards drawn.
- Use the "Mixed Topping Pizza" (page 149) and have students color the various toppings instead of only the pepperoni.

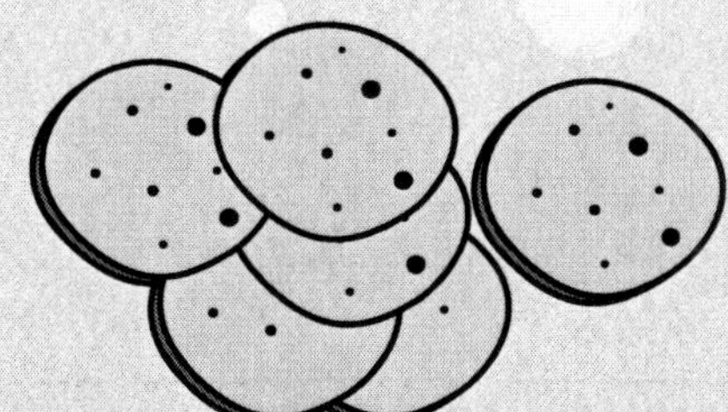

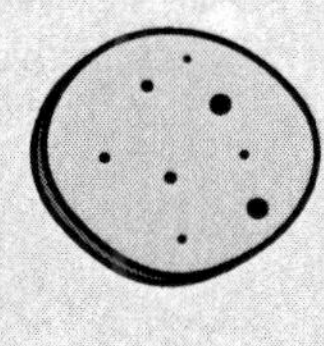

Pizza Pattern

Mixed Topping Pizza

Disappearing Stars

Skill:

Subtracting

Suggested Group Size:

2–6 students

Activity Overview:

Students erase stars from a night scene, based on subtraction problems.

Materials:

- whiteboard or chalkboard
- dry erase markers and eraser
- two dice

Activity Preparation

1. Draw 20 stars on a whiteboard or chalkboard.

Activity Procedure

1. Have a student roll the dice and determine the difference between the two numbers. He or she then erases the same number of stars as the difference between the two dice.

2. Have other students take turns following the same procedure. The game is over when all the stars have been erased from the board. When only a few stars remain on the board, the subtraction problem answer must be the exact number as the number of stars remaining on the board.

Adaptations

- Use the 0–6 number cards (pages 168–170) at the back of this book instead of dice.
- Use one die and have the students erase the same number of stars as the number shown on the die.
- Draw other nighttime objects on the board that can also be erased.
- Draw a garden of flowers. The flowers that are erased are ones that got "picked" by the students.

5-3=2

The Big Scoop

Skill:

Subtracting

Suggested Group Size:

2–4 students

Activity Overview:

Students create subtraction problems by scooping connecting cubes out of a pail.

Materials:

- "Subtraction Recording Sheet" (page 154)
- 10 connecting cubes
- small beach pail
- small shovel
- pad of sticky notes
- marker

Activity Preparation

1. Photocopy "Subtraction Recording Sheet," one per student, on regular or cardstock paper (or print copies from the CD).
2. Place 10 connecting cubes in the beach pail.
3. Write the number 10 on a sticky note and attach it to the front of the beach pail.

Activity Procedure

1. Give each student a recording sheet.
2. Place the pail and shovel in a central location.
3. Tell the students that the sticky note on the front of the pail has the number of cubes in the pail written on it.
4. Have a student use the shovel to scoop out some cubes from the pail.
5. Have the student count how many cubes were scooped out of the pail. He or she then records a subtraction problem on the recording sheet to show how many cubes are still in the pail.
6. Continue following the same procedure until each child's recording sheet is completed.

Adaptations

- Have students take two scoops out of the pail and record the problem.
- Place 20 connecting cubes in the pail. Have students take two scoops of cubes out of the pail and add the numbers together. Provide "Addition Recording Sheet" (page 155) for students to record the problem.
- Have the students close their eyes. Take some cubes out of the pail. Have students determine how many cubes you took out of the pail, based on how many are still in the pail.
- Students may check their answers by counting the remaining cubes in the pail.

Subtraction Recording Sheet

1. __________ - __________ = __________

2. __________ - __________ = __________

3. __________ - __________ = __________

4. __________ - __________ = __________

5. __________ - __________ = __________

Addition Recording Sheet

1. ________ + ________ = ________

2. ________ + ________ = ________

3. ________ + ________ = ________

4. ________ + ________ = ________

5. ________ + ________ = ________

Skill:

Subtracting

Suggested Group Size:

2–4 students

Activity Overview:

Students solve subtraction problems and then move space markers that represent animals parachuting to the ground.

Materials:

- "Parachuting Animals Game Mats" (pages 158–159)
- two dice
- beans, buttons, or other space markers

Activity Preparation

1. Photocopy "Parachuting Animals Game Mats," one per student, on cardstock paper (or print color copies from the CD).
2. Cut each page of the game mats on the dotted lines to create individual game mats.
3. Laminate the game mats for durability.

Activity Procedure

1. Give each student a game mat and a space marker.
2. Have the students place the space markers on each animal's shirt.
3. Have a student roll the dice and determine the difference between the two numbers rolled. If the student answers the problem correctly, he or she may move his or her space marker the number of spaces indicated on the dice, in a downward direction on the two ladders. If the student does not answer the problem correctly, the space marker remains where it is and the next student takes a turn.
4. Have other students take turns, following the same procedure. When only a few spaces remain, the subtraction problem answer must equal the exact number needed to get to the ground. The activity is over once all of the animals have "landed on the ground."

Adaptations

- Use only one die and change the activity into a counting game. The number rolled is the number of spaces a marker is moved.
- Photocopy the game mat on regular paper. Omit the space markers. Allow students to color the number of spaces that match either the number rolled or the difference between the two numbers rolled.
- Allow students to play multiple game mats at the same time. Students may also use the number on each die separately to move more than one animal closer to the ground during their turns; –e.g., if a difference is determined to be 3, then a student may move his or her space marker 2 on the rabbit and 1 on the bear.)

Parachuting Animals Game Mat

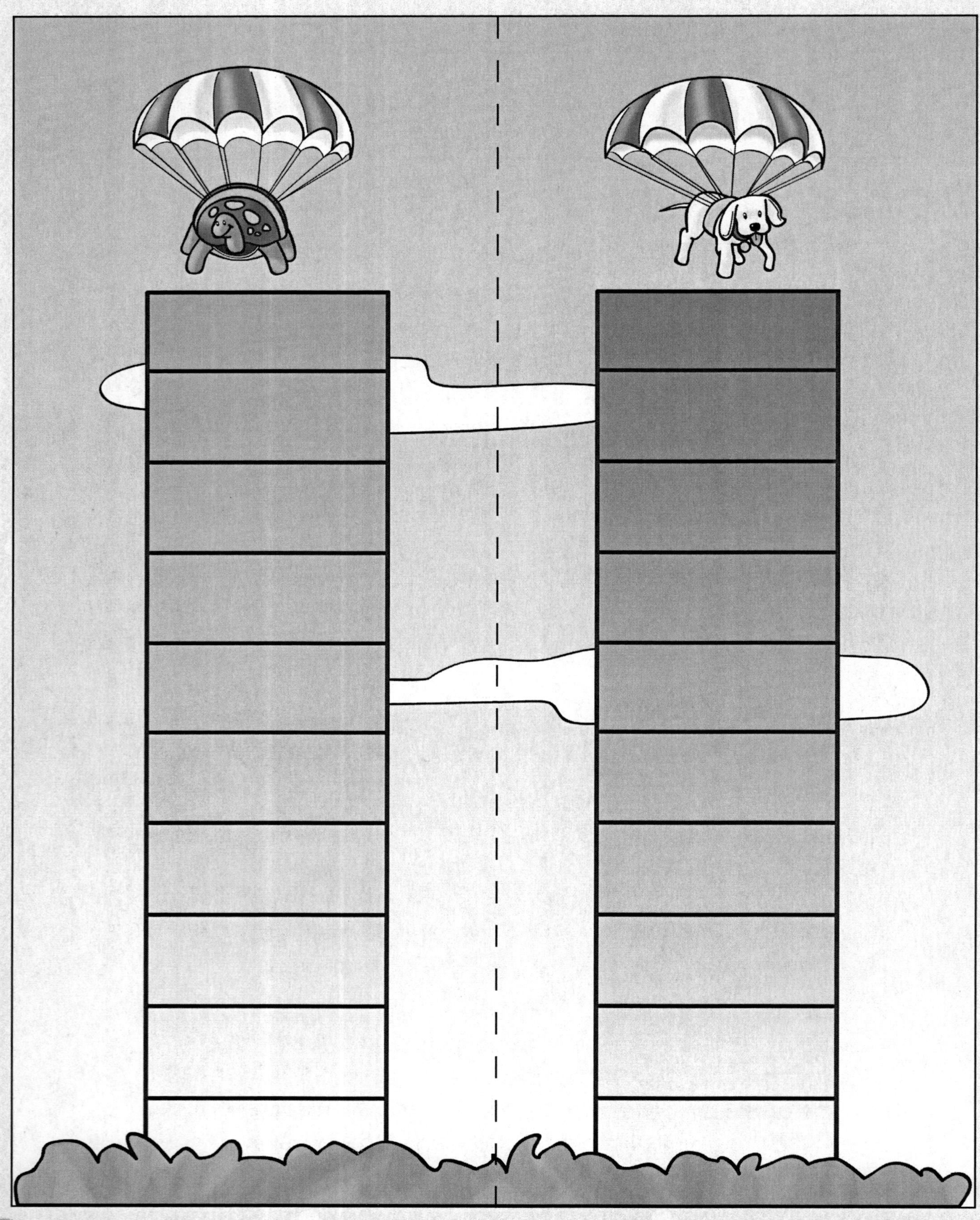

Parachuting Animals Game Mat (cont.)

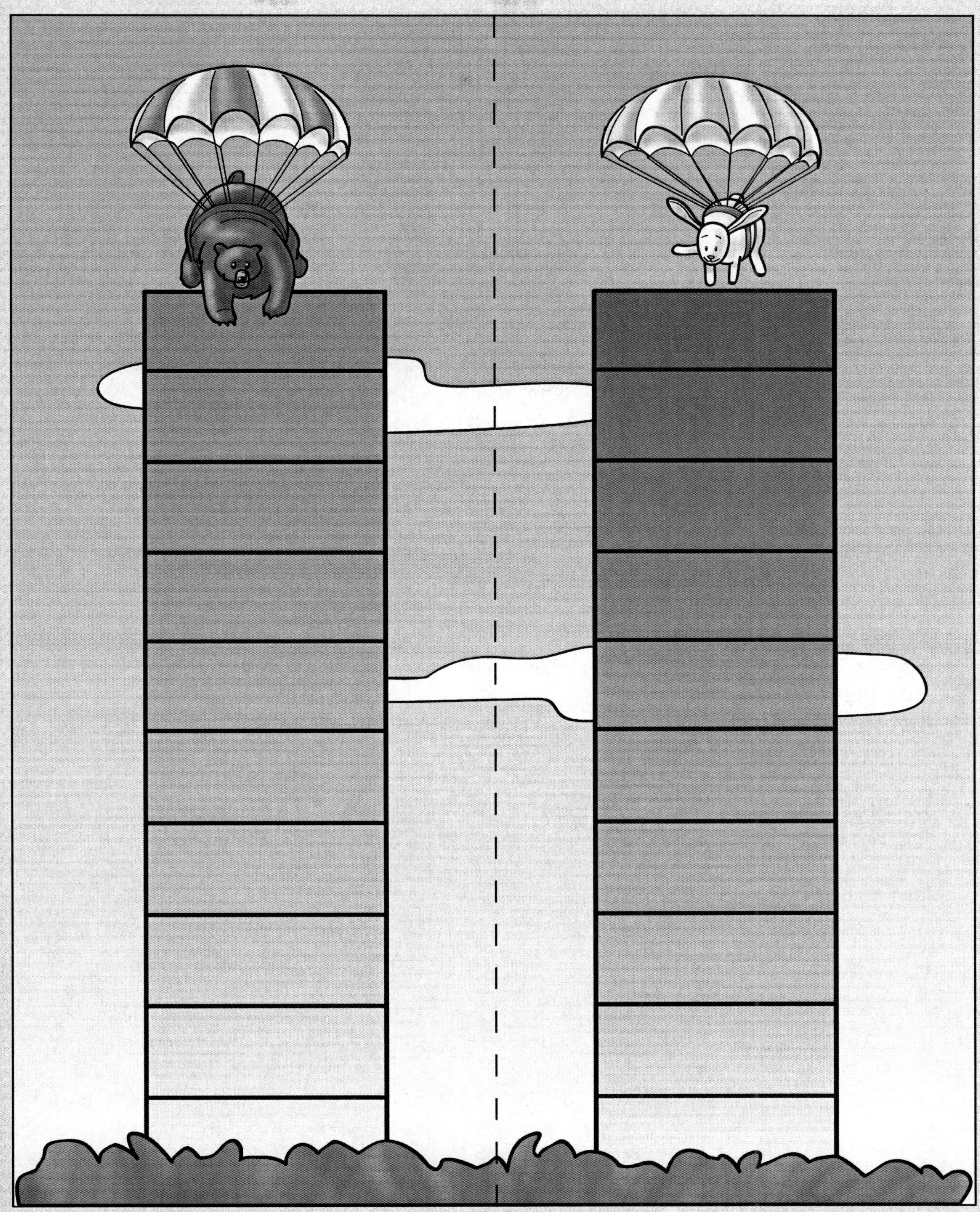

Egg Carton Shake

Skill:

Subtracting

Suggested Group Size:

2–4 students

Activity Overview:

Students shake an egg carton and subtract the number written in the egg carton compartment from the number written on the top of the egg carton.

Materials:

- "Egg Carton Numbers" (page 162)
- egg cartons
- button or other space marker

Activity Preparation

1. Photocopy "Egg Carton Numbers" on cardstock paper (or print color copies from the CD).
2. Cut out the 0–5 circles from the top portion of the page.
3. Glue the numbered circles inside the compartments of an egg carton, one number per compartment.
4. Place a button or other space marker in the egg carton and close the lid.
5. Write a number between six and ten on the lid of the egg carton.
6. Create several egg carton games following the same preparation procedure. Write a different number on the lid of each egg carton.

1. Provide a student with an egg carton.
2. Have the student shake the egg carton and open the lid.
3. Have the student say the name of the number in the same compartment as the space maker. Have the student subtract that number from the number on the lid of the egg carton.
4. Allow other students to take turns, following the same procedure. Continue the game until each student has had five turns, or as time allows.

Adaptations

- Create egg carton games using the bottom portion of "Egg Carton Numbers" (page 162). Write a number greater than 11 on the lid of the egg carton. Have students practice subtracting with larger numbers.
- Omit writing a number on the egg carton lid. Have the students practice identifying the number in the same compartment as the space marker.
- Omit writing a number on the egg carton lid. Place two space markers in the egg carton. Have the students add the numbers together.
- Create egg carton games using "Egg Carton Subtraction" (page 163) or "Egg Carton Addition" (page 164). Have students say the answer to the problem that is in the same compartment as their space markers.

Egg Carton Numbers

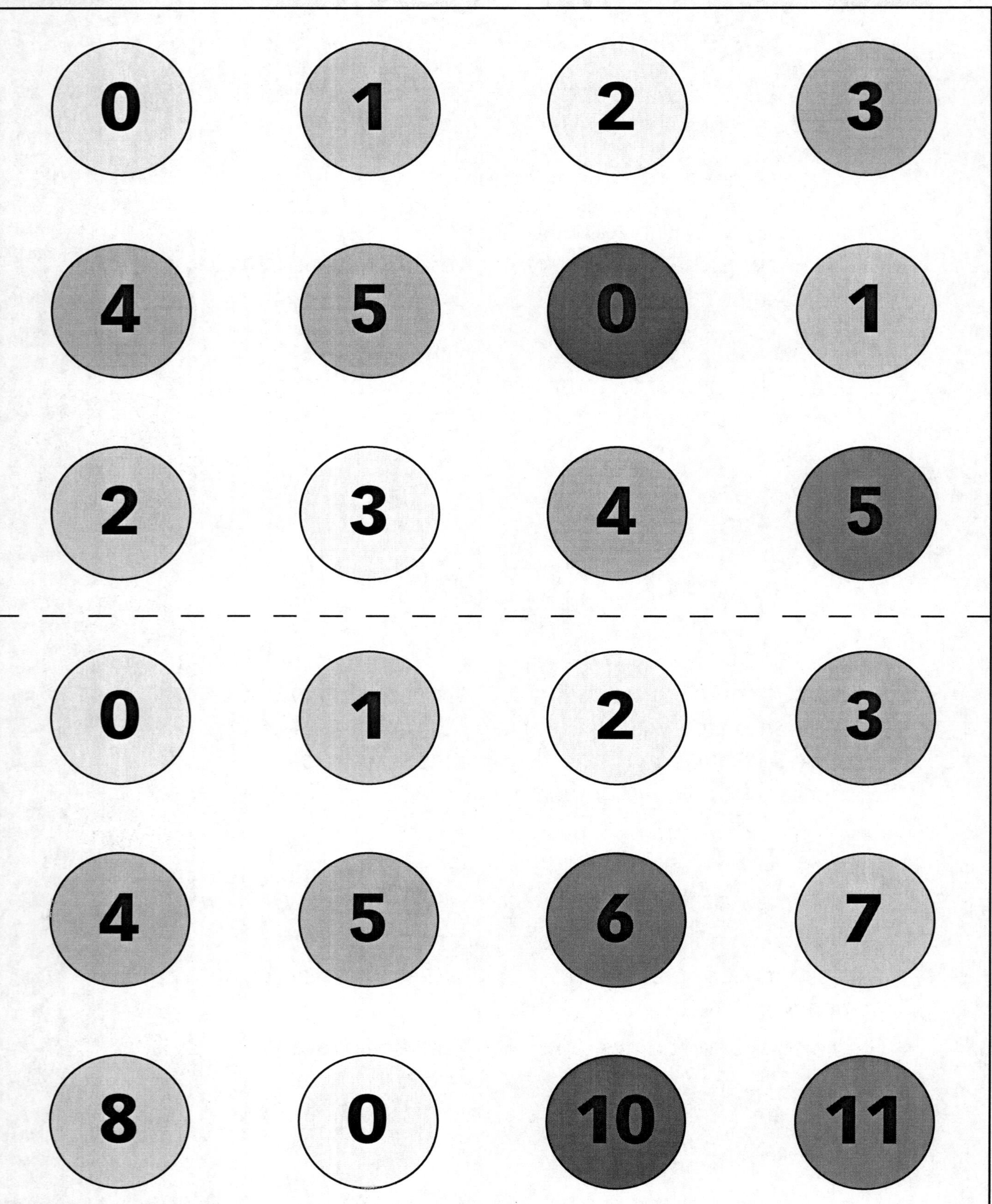

Egg Carton Subtraction

Select 12 problems for use in the egg carton game.

1-0	1-1	2-0	2-1
2-2	3-0	3-1	3-2
3-3	4-0	4-1	4-2
4-3	4-4	5-0	5-1
5-2	5-3	5-4	5-5

Egg Carton Addition

Select 12 problems for use in the egg carton game.

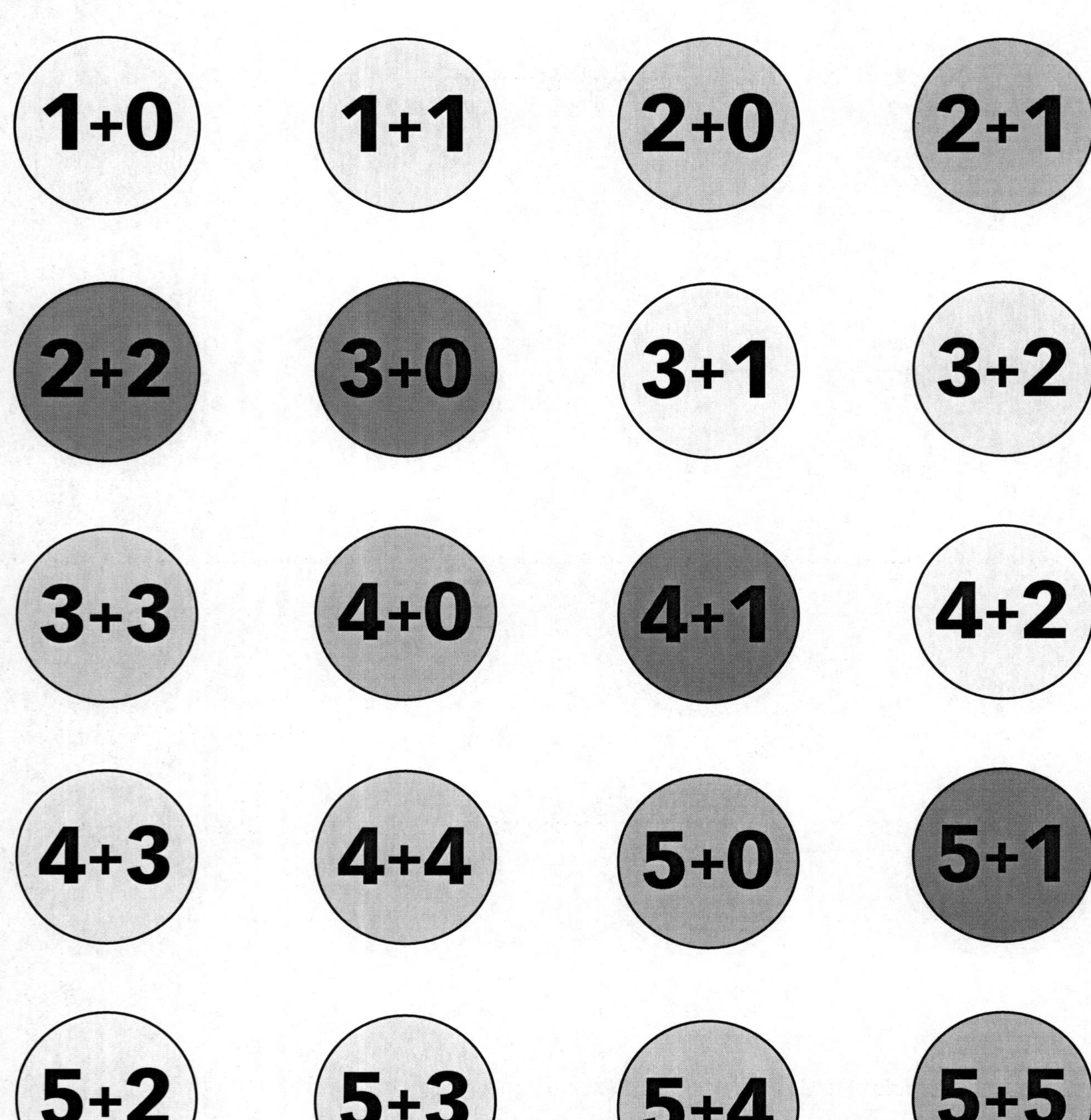

References Cited

Allen, K. E. 1979. Early math experiences and the facilitative adult. ERIC Document ED192863.

Buehler, R. M.C. 1992. Making school fun for you and your students. ERIC Document ED349302.

Burk, D. Math in a box. 1992. *Instructor* 101 (6): 39–41.

Burns, M. 1998. *Math: Facing an American phobia.* Sausalito: Math Solutions Publications.

Goldberg, S. 1990. Developing and implementing a parental awareness program to enhance children's mathematics performance and attitude. ERIC Document ED327383.

Guha, S. 2000. Eyes to see and ears to hear: Teaching math in the childhood years. Integrating math in children's learning centers. ERIC Document ED438177.

Kanter, P. F., and Darby, Linda B. 1999. Helping your child learn math. ERIC Document ED431636.

Moss, J. 1997. Math that makes sense. *Learning* (January/February): 52–56.

Onslow, B. 1990. Overcoming conceptual obstacles: The qualified use of a game. *School Science and Mathematics* (November): 581–92.

Perry, P. J. 1997 Guide to math materials: Resources to support the NCTM. ERIC Document ED405204.

Summer, G. L. 1994. Take-me-home activity packets: Parent-child games for learning. ERIC Document ED420385.

Wakefield, A. P. 1997. Supporting math thinking. *Phi Delta Kappan* (November): 233–236.

Willoughby, S. S. 1981. Elementary school mathematics: The real basics. *Momentum* 12 (4): 17–20.

Shape Cards

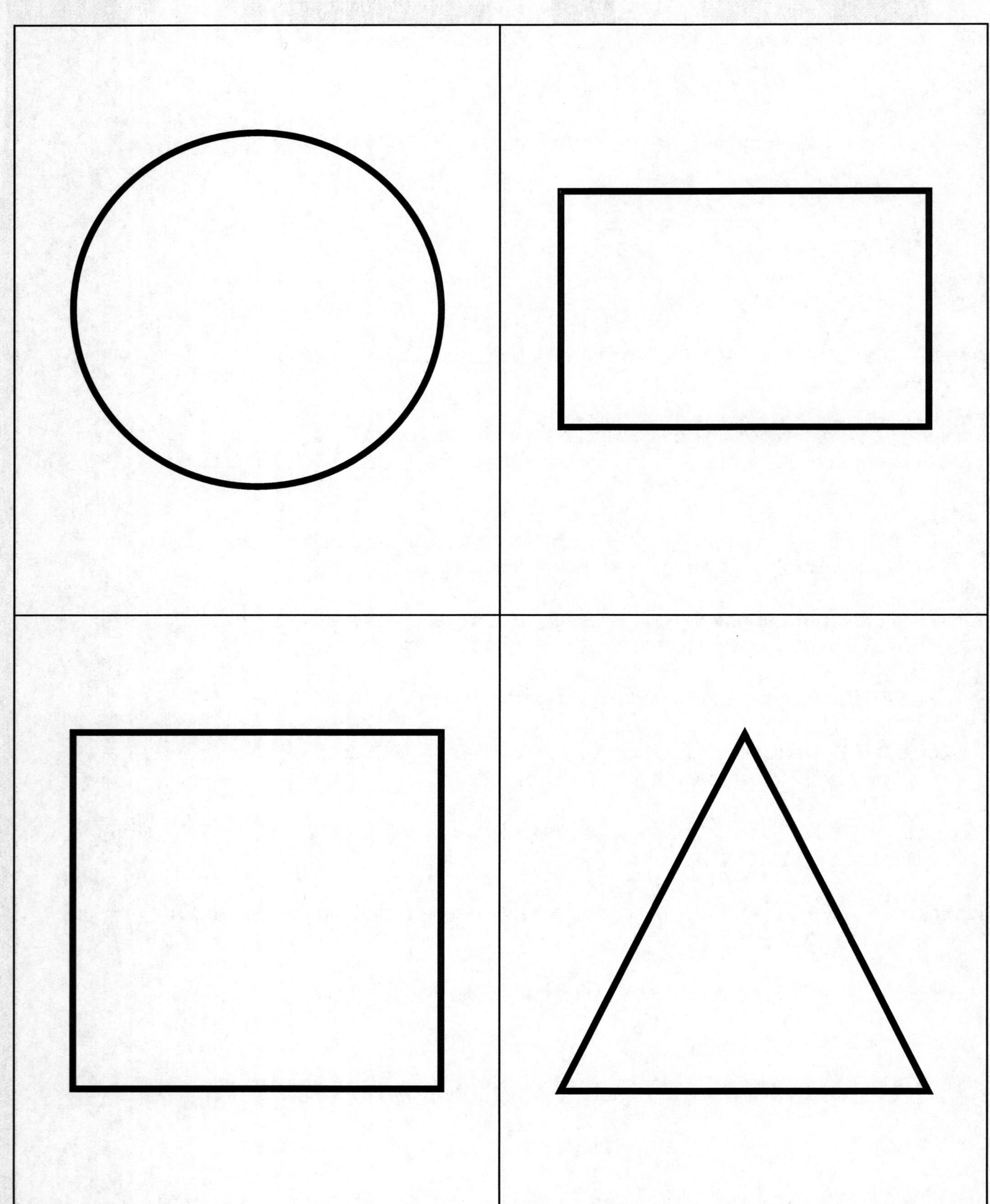

Shape Cards (cont.)

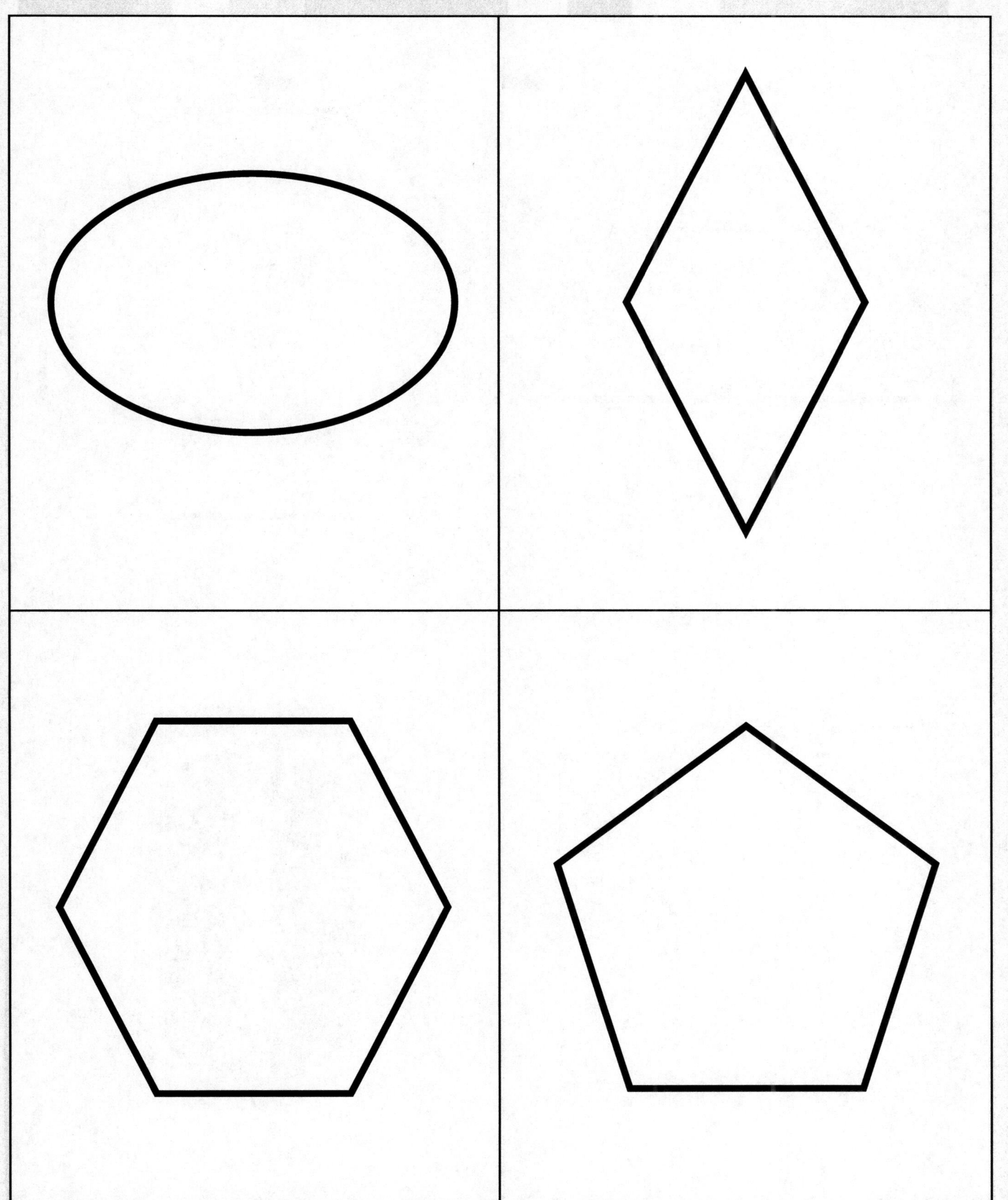

Shape Cards (cont.)/Number Card

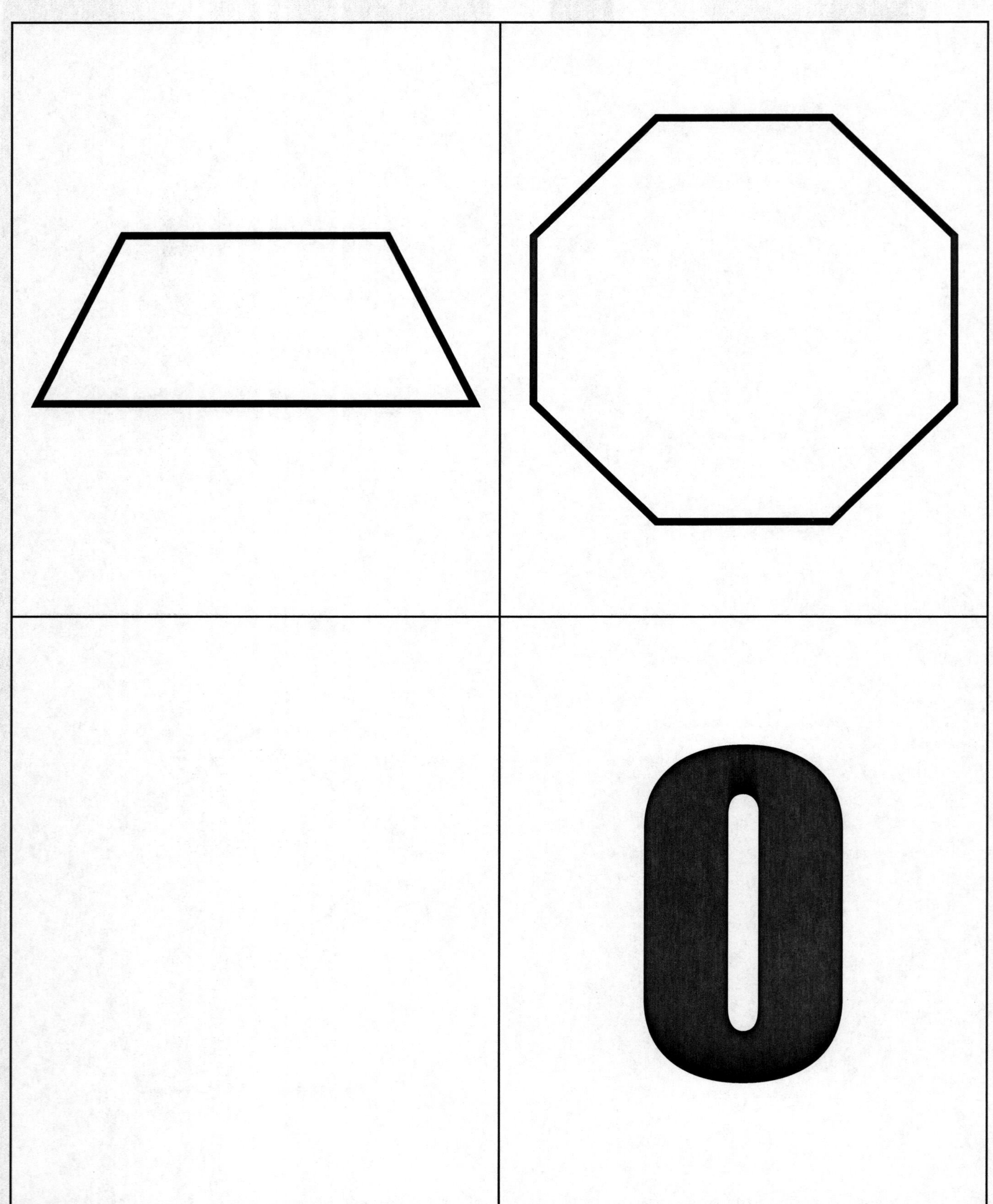

Number Cards (cont.)

1	2
3	4

Number Cards (cont.)

5	6
7	8

Number Cards (cont.)

9	10
11	12

Number Cards (cont.)

13	14
15	16

Number Cards (cont.)

17	18
19	20

Number Words

one	**two**
three	**four**

Number Words (cont.)

five	six
seven	eight

Number Words (cont.)

nine	ten